ENERGY SECRETS

ANTONIA HARMAN

ENERGY SECRETS

HOW TO LIVE TO YOUR FULL POTENTIAL

yellow kite

First published in Great Britain in 2023 by Yellow Kite
An imprint of Hodder & Stoughton
An Hachette UK company

1

A CIP catalogue record for this title is available from the British Library

Hardback ISBN 9781399719384
eBook ISBN 9781399719391

Typeset in Celeste by Hewer Text UK Ltd, Edinburgh
Printed and bound in Great Britain by Clays Ltd, Elcograf S.p.A.

Hodder & Stoughton policy is to use papers that are natural, renewable and recyclable products and made from wood grown in sustainable forests. The logging and manufacturing processes are expected to conform to the environmental regulations of the country of origin.

Yellow Kite
Hodder & Stoughton Ltd
Carmelite House
50 Victoria Embankment
London EC4Y 0DZ

www.yellowkitebooks.co.uk

I dedicate this book to YOU for taking a chance on me and for your willingness to explore the magic within.

Spiritual evolution is for warriors, wizards and lion hearts, old souls dedicated to peace, harmony and happiness. Those willing to explore and adapt for the betterment of themselves and humanity. I salute YOU, dear reader.

Contents

Introduction

Do you intuitively know that there is more to life? Do you feel in your bones that it's not meant to be this hard? Is the constant grind grating at your soul? Do you feel spiritually out of alignment? If so, you have come to the right place. This book will let you in on energy secrets and ancient wisdom with a modern twist, to help you connect and attract the life you desire, the life you deserve.

Happiness and abundance are your birthright, and they are closer than you think. This book will provide you with easy steps to improve your life exponentially, minor tweaks to your actions and thinking that will make a world of difference.

There have always been 'lucky' people in the world who seem to have it all, gliding through life looking as if they don't even need to try. If you are ready to become one of the lucky few, keep reading!

I believe in working smarter, not harder. Aligning and attracting as opposed to pursuing. Your dreams and best life shouldn't be running from you; they don't need chasing. It makes more sense to entice and draw in your heart's desires. There will always be work to do, but the work can be fun and rewarding.

I invite you to see the world through new eyes. To learn tips and techniques to help you breeze through challenges. To better understand who you are, why things may be going wrong and how to correct course. To help you connect more to nature and your intuition and ultimately to find happiness.

This book contains wisdom and a-ha moments that will help you join the dots. Simple yet ground-breaking formulas to guide you. Tips and tricks that are easy to implement and incorporate into your routine.

I merge the physical with the metaphysical in a digestible way. There is something here for everyone, from people new to spirituality and tentatively dipping their toes in to well-versed aficionados.

For those who don't know me, I'm Antonia Harman from Divine Empowerment. I am a multi-award-winning, internationally renowned healer, teacher and wizard (more on that later). As a child, I was intuitive, even psychic, but never really explored that part of myself. Then, in 2007, everything changed. While I was on a walk with my friend Lucie, she collapsed in the street in agony. She had a burst eardrum and was waiting for surgery (which was costly and had no guarantee of success); in the meantime, she was experiencing ongoing stabbing pain. I took her into the loos of a restaurant and placed my hands on her ears. I can only describe what I did as pulling out blocked energy from them. Her earache instantly vanished, and she has never experienced it since. She didn't have (or need) the surgery. This was my eureka moment, my epiphany: at that moment, I knew that there was more to healing than modern medicine, and, in some cases, a scalpel simply can't help!

This event sent me down rabbit holes; I started ferociously exploring the world of energy healing. As strange as it may sound, I have spent an enormous proportion of the last two decades in a trance state, accruing wisdom and healing abilities straight from the universe. I was told recently that saints spend more time on their backs than on their knees. Now I'm no saint, but it does make sense that upgrading your DNA and spiritually and physically evolving will take a toll on your body. The trances I experience are deep meditation. I can feel energy pulsating through my body; they take a physical toll too. There are times when my brain won't function at all and I feel like a zombie. Basic tasks seem insurmountable. My body pain is often excruciating, a bit like after a very hard workout but relentless. My fatigue was so extreme a few years ago that I couldn't even get out of bed. To feed myself, I would have to crawl to the stairs, shimmy down them on my bottom, and then crawl again to the kitchen. I would hoist myself up to switch the kettle on and then crumple onto the floor.

This went on for years. It would be easy to assume that I had chronic fatigue syndrome or a similar illness. The unique thing about my journey is that if I had a commitment such as a dear friend's birthday, I would feel fine and have the energy to see them, go for dinner, even dance – a luxury those with exhausting conditions such as chronic fatigue syndrome are not afforded. I could only do it once a month initially, then I was able to build it up to once a week, but if I chose carefully, I was still able to have a bit of a social life. The other unusual aspect of my experience is that after a bout of aching and exhaustion, I would have awakened new superpowers!

I have come to believe that we all have abilities beyond our current awareness. I would even go as far as to say we are gods and goddesses with amnesia – that's how powerful we are!

I have an online school where I teach my skills; all you have to do is simply watch videos loaded with magic and follow along (in your pyjamas, if you like!), and you will awaken your latent superpowers. We have a wonderfully supportive community and regular meetings. I work with people both individually and in large groups (currently up to about 20,000 and it will expand more). I'm best known for instantly dissolving emotional trauma, although I have discovered how to successfully heal what I believe underpins various more minor ailments and even serious dis-eases (see chapter 9 for my Grand Theory of Dis-ease). I am sought out by people with a multitude of illnesses, including those in the limelight. Everyone gets sick, has emotional ups and downs and needs help from time to time.

I love healing people. It's the most rewarding thing in the world to see someone who has been in pain for decades heal in minutes or even seconds. I've helped countless people release their vicious cycle of pain and trauma. In my experience, stagnated emotions are the root of all dis-ease. Release the emotions, and you will be amazed at how much better your life becomes.

My favourite part of my job, though, is seeing my students perform mind-blowing work. A few years ago, a group of nine of my students worked together to lift a fellow student's depression. To this day, it has never returned. The fact that my students performed this healing makes it feel to me all the more wonderful and rewarding.

Classes are always full of mini miracles. I teach hundreds of energy techniques to solve a multitude of issues. To give a couple of examples: unwinding the fascia (the body's connective tissue, which can tense up from emotional or physical assault) can diminish or even solve long-term pain and tightness. I have seen the full range of motion in someone's neck restored after years of stiffness and agony, and a woman's chronic pain, from giving birth two decades prior instantly disappear.

My advanced practitioners and I work a lot on increasing lung capacity, which can be affected by sorrow, sadness and grief and manifest as anxiety and panic. We work on energetically deleting people's sorrow, sadness and grief, in concert with breathwork. Without the emotions clogging up their lungs, I have seen people's lung capacity double or even triple in seconds. It's pretty profound.

> 'Any sufficiently advanced form of technology is indistinguishable from magic.'
>
> Arthur C. Clarke

Magic is within each and every one of us. It is all around you and, more importantly, inside of you. Supernormal abilities are possible and YOU are far more awesome than you know. A great example of this is Wim Hof, who performs 'impossible' feats like climbing Mount Everest in shorts.

I strongly believe that what I call ascended abilities are achievable. Underneath all your trauma, pain, suffering and energetic blocks, awaits your true divine self. It's my belief that our energy systems have severely atrophied and that long ago we really were gods and goddesses. What I mean here is that I believe the legends of Atlantis, and stories of the gods from traditions including the Ancient Norse, Roman, Greek, Meso-American, Hindu and all the others, are stories of real people – they just happened long ago. So, we have the blueprints and potential to ourselves be enlightened beings, AKA gods!

There are accounts of people demonstrating the sort of abilities you see in a Marvel or DC movie – for example, being able to heal, liquefy stone and walk on water. 'Spiritual superpowers' on this level are traditionally called 'siddhis' and they are certainly profound and relatively rare, but they are not exclusive to only a few people; according to Chinese and Tibetan written history, nearly 200,000 monks have achieved this enlightened state. There are accounts from India of many enlightened yogis too. This phenomenon is referred to in spiritual circles as achieving a rainbow body.

Ancient Egyptian mystery schools also had (fairly brutal) ways to achieve enlightenment; to ascend, you needed firstly to let go of all of your trauma. This meant initiations, including activities like swimming across crocodile-infested waters.

Some of this is perhaps not within our understanding in our modern Western context, but the principle – that to ascend you must be able to conquer fear and stand in your power, and be brave no matter what is happening around you – absolutely stands and, I'm sure, will resonate with you.

If you are ready to become who you were always destined to be, this book contains the first keys!

My motivation for writing this book is to share a lifetime of discoveries, to help you glide through life more blissfully and become divinely empowered. This book, and what you can learn from it, will help you through hard times, help you find peace among chaos and make sense of the seen and unseen world, the world of energy and magic.

Let this book guide you to feel more at peace with yourself and the world, happier and more comfortable within your own skin.

Please highlight the tips and sections that resonate most deeply so you can easily refer back to them – my favourite books are filled with sticky notes and scribbles.

Some of what you read here may feel a little strange or even uncomfortable initially, but please do delve into it with an open heart and mind. It's my hope that this book will enrich the lives of those you care about – and your own!

I am so grateful to you for reading my book. I'm trusting the universe that this is the perfect time to share the knowledge I have accrued over my life. We are entering what mystics have prophesied as 'The Golden Age', the time when kindness, love, truth and integrity will become the fundamentals we base our lives upon. I believe that energy healing is the future of medicine – so in reading my words you will have a head start!

I hope this book helps your life become even just a little brighter and a touch more magical. Also, that you use the skills you will garner to help and heal yourself and your friends and loved ones; that it will help your world become softer and more manageable.

Enjoy!

With love and kindness, peace, truth and happiness!

Antonia xx

CHAPTER ONE

Fight, Flight and Stress

Let's face it, the current state of the world is stressful! Stress was ramped up considerably for all of us during the worst of the Covid pandemic and has barely stabilised, let alone subsided. Not being able to see loved ones and the intense and upsetting news cycles, not to mention ever-changing guidelines, took a toll on our mental health. As I write this, there is worry over a possible nuclear war; Armageddon is on the horizon. There is a cost-of-living crisis that has meant that many people have had to choose between eating or heating their home. Then there's your home life: you may be overcommitted with social and family obligations, working to cram as much into your free time as possible, milking every last moment

of the weekend or your holiday before you return to work. Then you have your job, and the work environment, maybe involving never-ending deadlines, politics with colleagues, stress and drama. It's a lot, and it's all-consuming. There is little time for you and your passions and desires.

A survey by the Mental Health Foundation tells us that 74 per cent of people in the UK have felt overwhelmed or unable to cope at some point in the last year.[1] That means that three-quarters of Brits are feeling the pressure. Worse, 32 per cent of the adults surveyed said they had experienced suicidal feelings due to stress. Sixteen per cent of the adults questioned said that they had self-harmed as a result of stress. These are truly horrifying statistics. In this chapter, I will break down how your body responds to stress, look at what's actually going on internally and offer plenty of advice to help you minimise stress and live a more peaceful existence.

In order for you to protect, nurture and improve your energy you need, first, to understand how to read it and how to guard it. This means understanding what triggers energy depletion for you versus what leads to nurturing and enhancing your energy. To encourage a life of peace and contentment, with a spring in your step and a joie de vivre; and on the other hand to learn what leaves you feeling flat and drained.

This chapter will teach you how to self-regulate. How your nervous system and stress mechanisms work. Ways to stimulate your parasympathetic (relaxed) nervous system, how to live stress-free and how to encourage more joy and high-vibrational living into your life.

You will find that increasing your energy and guarding it becomes infectious – once you know how to do this, you will no longer want to spend time around people who deplete your energy and leave you empty. You will gravitate, instead, towards people, activities and experiences that leave you feeling full of life and full of energy and enrich your soul. You will become the captain of your ship.

While life can, of course, throw you curveballs, how you react to them, and your outlook and approach are something you have total control over. I will teach you techniques covering all of these areas and will give you actionable takeaways, so you can thrive, feel empowered and feed your energy rather than watch it deplete.

Think of your life. Do you feel that you experience moments of zen – peace, tranquillity? Are they frequent? Are you living harmoniously? Do you sometimes feel that you are living on the edge of impending anxiety or worry? I'm going to talk about four extreme states of being (also known as trauma responses) that you may or may not be too familiar with. For example, you have probably heard of and may well have experienced fight-or-flight mode, but have you heard of and would you recognise the experience of freeze or flop?

I want to explain each of these extreme states, so you

have the power to know the difference between them and to be able to spot them the next time they creep up on you. Being aware of these extreme states is incredibly important – you need to understand your body and your emotions and what they're trying to tell you. If you are to protect your energy, you must first understand what is triggering your body to deplete it. Stress exhausts your energy and compromises your immune system; conversely, laughter and peace strengthen it. This means that living a calm existence will help you stay healthy!

The five trauma responses, which come into play when we are facing impending danger, are: fight, flight, freeze, flop and friend.

Fight includes physically fighting, pushing, struggling, shouting, saying 'NO!', etc. People report feeling an almost superhuman strength that allows them to fight an attacker who may be bigger, stronger and/or more skilled than them. If you have had training in self-defence or martial arts, this can come in handy here as your automatic response will be enhanced by your learned skills.

Flight is when you physically get away from the threat. It includes running, hiding or backing away. A horse galloping away from a perceived threat is one example of the flight response.

Freeze is when you get stuck where you are and can't move. This can happen when you are crossing a road and suddenly a car appears out of nowhere; you may find your feet seem glued to the street. People also freeze, go tense, still and silent, during sexual assault. This is not giving consent, it's an instinctive survival response. It's common for animals to freeze in the face of danger to avoid fights and harm. They may also 'play dead' to avoid being eaten by predators.

Flop is when your legs buckle underneath you, and it's why people suggest you sit down to hear bad news. Your muscles become loose and your body floppy. When you are floppy, you are less likely to sustain injury from an attack. It also lessens pain. Additionally, your mind may shut down as a protective mechanism.

Friend is when you call for help; this could be from a passer-by or sometimes even the assailant – you may attempt to placate, negotiate, plead or bribe them. This, again, is not giving consent – it's a survival mechanism.

These built-in survival mechanisms happen naturally and spontaneously and, when facing danger, you will experience one or another.

The less stress you have, the more at peace you will be. When you are stressed or upset the world is a far more brutal place. Anger attracts anger and stress attracts stress. The more upset you are, the more magnetic you become for more of the same (there is more on this in the manifesting chapter). The happier you are, the more happiness finds you. Understanding and processing stress is crucial to living your best life. Stress is also utterly exhausting! So, if you want to have the energy to do the things you love, it's best avoided. Remember, it is vital, when any issues do crop up, that you talk them out and deal with them in the moment – the longer you leave problems, the more they fester and grow, and the worse it all becomes.

Now for how it works. What all of these responses mean in our modern context and how they affect your body and mind. The stress response requires a lot of energy, but it is the wrong sort of energy and it could be better spent doing more pleasurable activities.

Humans are designed to live a calm, harmonious existence in synergy with nature. No stress, no drama and in a relaxed state. In an ideal world, dangers should be few and far between. Unless you are a president or have a super-stressful job, your life should be far easier than it currently is, pretty much plain sailing, with only the occasional 'eek' moment. We modern people have far more resources than humans in the past, as well as the greatest level of safety and comfort in recorded history. So, life should be a breeze!

In the developed world at least, thankfully, people rarely starve, most have roofs over their heads and invasion from rival tribes is rare. We live better than monarchs would have done a few hundred years ago, with easy access to infinite libraries of information and music, which, in the past, were only accessible to the rich. There was no lighting, indoor plumbing, let alone electricity.

Arguably, we are living in the most privileged and prosperous time in history; but disease and mental-health decline are rapidly on the increase.

Why? The main reason we are falling apart is stress, which is caused by the actions of the sympathetic nervous system.

The sympathetic nervous system is one division of the autonomic nervous system, which regulates our involuntary physiologic processes, including heart rate, blood pressure, breathing (respiration), digestion and sexual arousal. When a stressful situation activates the sympathetic nervous system, adrenaline, cortisol and noradrenaline course through our veins, causing our muscles to tense, our heartbeat and breath to quicken, increased sweating and sensory perception (for example, enhanced hearing) and a rise in blood pressure, so the blood can get to the muscles in the limbs and allow them to move as fast as possible and with maximum strength to either fight back against the danger or get away from it.

This is, just as it sounds, a huge amount of stress for your mind, body and soul to undergo. When you are stressed, your body cannot rest or sleep properly, it's harder to digest food, and very little bodily rejuvenation happens. This makes sense from a purely survival-focused point of view; when we are faced with danger, survival is the critical priority and the rest can wait. You may have noticed that people who are anxious often have IBS and other digestive issues; this is because blood and energy are diverted away from their guts to the periphery (the limbs) in anticipation of having to run or fight.

Under stress, your IQ even goes down. A study at Georgetown University in the USA created a 'stress index' using a sample of 4,000 seven-year-old children and found that those who had little to no stress had on average an IQ of 104, while their more stressed counterparts averaged 91.[2]

The drop in IQ makes sense from a pure survival point of view; in the face of imminent danger there are no complex conundrums to consider, just getting away or defending yourself. Instinct and decisive action will serve you better than pondering and considering. Blood is diverted away from your brain to your arms and legs so that you can deal with the threat.

The sympathetic nervous system is perfect in design; it is intended, and allows us, to face threats to our lives. The problem is with us and the way we currently live.

What happens when we are exposed to stress on a constant long-term basis? Imagine a quaint, picturesque little village. People growing crops, and tending to animals. They study and think, and the pace of life is slow and easygoing. It's an expansive, relaxed existence. They accrue more land and resources. Food is bountiful; their homes are a cornucopia of fruits, vegetables, grains, and meat, so much so that plenty can be put aside for the colder seasons and rainy days.

Suddenly they hear an air-raid siren and see planes overhead. The enemy is close. They are in clear and present danger. They run into their cellars to hide.

Providing they are not bombed, they stay safe in their cellars for hours, days or even weeks. They are depleting resources but these are abundant, so it's not insurmountable. The problems come if they have to stay there for prolonged periods. They are eating their stocks, decreasing their reserves and are not able to tend to the land to cultivate more food. If this shrinking of assets continues, they will have nothing left.

This is what happens when you are continuously stressed. You are taking from the pot without adding to it, which results in every bodily system operating below par much of the time. As well as IQ, the immune system is compromised. A study suggests that one minute of anger weakens the immune system for four to five hours.[3] Amazingly, one minute of laughter boosts it for 24 hours. Although it doesn't always feel that way, the universe is positively orientated.

Of course, it's not all doom and gloom and energy depletion. There are hundreds of ways you can break out of trauma responses; there are simple, actionable changes you can make to your life, to ensure that you have clarity and an abundance of energy and are living more harmoniously despite the influence of modern-day pressures in our fast-paced world. I'm going to give you some simple tips to start implementing in your daily life. As you work on them, note how you feel, see which ones work best for you.

Before you start, you need to know exactly how the

other side of the nervous system works and how it can help you. You need to be aware of what triggers your trauma responses. The parasympathetic nervous system is how you 'rest and digest'. When you are relaxed, your blood and energy return to your trunk (torso), where all your organs are. Your body has a chance to heal and replenish itself. More blood and energy are available to your brain and organs, which boosts your IQ. Anxiety decreases, you worry less and sleep better, you are more present, living from the now rather than preparing for impending doom. When you sleep better, you function better, regardless of what life throws at you.

Stress is closely correlated with illness because when you are stressed, your body doesn't have the bandwidth for maintenance, so any weaknesses you may have become more apparent, which can, unfortunately, lead to illness.

Keep track of how you feel each day for seven days – when are you triggered and what causes it? When do you feel empowered? When are you feeling like you may be in fight-or-flight mode? Have you frozen, flopped or called for help? You will clearly be able to see the pattern of what is causing your energy to feel off kilter. This knowledge will help you make the changes you need to address these energy-depleting issues.

ENERGY HACK

Believe it or not, your lips have parasympathetic nerve fibres running through them.

Next time you feel stressed or anxious, take a few moments to softly rub your lips with a finger or two. Gently caress your lips, focusing on the sensation, and notice your mind and body relax.

Kissing is another way to soothe your nerves, for the same reason. If you happen to be with your partner when anxiety strikes, give kissing a go!

Kissing, hugging and any form of loving touch (with humans or animals) induces the production of oxytocin, the 'hugging hormone'. In other words, it gives you the warm and fuzzies, activating your parasympathetic nervous system.

When you are stressed, you tend to do shallow breathing – short, small breaths from the lungs, omitting the belly. Remember, stress causes you to live from your sympathetic nervous system. Unless you plan to wrap yourself up in cotton wool for the foreseeable future, stressful situations will occur. The trick is to not sweat the small stuff. Let go of old annoyances and grievances so they don't build up to the point where a minor inconvenience rattles you to the core. Also, learn how to bounce back fast: find inner peace by having the resolve to say no to negative thinking – choose to think about something positive. If you find yourself spiralling, get your body moving by dancing or taking a walk; nature is grounding and can quieten destructive thinking.

When someone says something catty, cold or demeaning, it's very easy to take it personally and to play the conversation on repeat like a broken record. Why did they say that? I must have really messed up. To assume they hate you and to build worst-case scenarios in your mind. Remember this liberating fact – it's NOT personal! People are wrapped up in their own emotions and traumas. They may get angry at you, but you are not really the trigger. The trigger is usually something that happened to them in the past. They are reliving an event that occurred when they were three or twenty-three.

You have the power to guard and protect your own energy; just because someone else is having a bad day, you don't need to inherit their energy. You have the right to thrive every single day. Realising it's not about you gives you the freedom to choose how to respond rather than react. There is no need to take on their stress and drama.

Keep your vibration high and stress-free. Don't gossip. Instead, spend your time building, creating and living in a positive mindset. The more positive, loving, kind, grateful and in service you are, the higher your vibration will be. You can't be stressed and happy or loving at the same time; they can't coexist, it's an impossibility. You can't raise your vibration if you are mixing in low-vibration circles where there is gossip and bad feeling.

What does it mean to be 'in service?'

Taking care of other people feels good. If you are ever emotionally low or anxious, go and help others. Donate some old clothes to charity, help at a jumble sale, volunteer in a kitchen for homeless people. When you help others, you feel internally wholesome and nourished. It ignites the warm fuzzies. Giving can feel better than receiving. Selfless service is part of spiritual development; taking the 'I' out of the situation helps too. The question should not be 'How can "I" help?' but rather 'What needs doing?' (Thinking in terms of the 'I' means your ego may get involved.) The motive behind your actions should be the greatest good for all, or, how can everybody win?

When these principles underpin your actions, you bring more light and love into the world and yourself.

It's very easy after a long day to want to put on a tracksuit, switch on the TV and physically relax; let's face it, after an exhausting day it can be difficult to find the energy to go for a walk, do a workout at home or head to the gym. However, movement can actually increase your energy, even if it's the last thing you want to do. Try to play it forwards – imagine how you will feel afterwards. Remember the saying 'you never regret a workout'! The same can be said for any physical movement.

The kinder you are to your body and nervous system, the better they will work for you. So go for a run or hit the gym, dance around the living room. Gentle exercise works too; you could go for a walk, do yoga or a few stretches; gardening has the added benefits of grounding you too, as you physically touch nature. Do whatever you love doing, just to get your body moving. If your form of body movement is fun for you, all the better: those happy hormones will flood your system and boost you into activating the parasympathetic nervous system.

Stress can cause premature and sudden ageing. You can see this clearly when people ascend to powerful roles. Presidents age ten years in four, and the same is true of many new parents. Of course, lack of sleep is probable in both scenarios, but both are highly stressful roles that demand a huge proportion of your energy resources.

Did you know that the best anti-ageing formula isn't created in a lab? It's not a super-expensive vitamin C serum or a collagen night mask. It's your attitude and how you tackle everything that life presents you with. The more stressed you are, the faster you will age, because you will force your body to work overtime and stop it from doing all of the incredible jobs it has to do to function to its full capacity.

Meditation or nourishing hobbies can slow the ageing process. I have seen people return from meditation retreats looking ten years younger!

There is more on meditation and meditation techniques later in the book. Meditation doesn't mean simply sitting in full lotus stilling the mind; there are many ways to meditate to suit your personal needs and abilities, ranging from retreats to in-person classes to online sessions.

Nourishing hobbies are ones where, after doing them, you feel connected and happy. Creating and making things is good for the soul: you could whittle wood, sew, knit, paint, bake or pursue some other creative endeavour.

You can feel proud of yourself when you create something, which is nourishing.

Finding an activity or hobby you love can also be nourishing, whether that be connecting to nature, swimming or paddling in the sea or a lake, even reading this book!

A messy home creates stress. You can never find anything, and the sight of it and the negative energy it creates in the house are irritating. Get organised, and throw things away that no longer serve you or bring you joy. If clothes don't fit, get rid of them – give them to friends, donate to charity or go along to a clothes-swapping event. At the very least, remove them from your wardrobe, bag them up and stick them in the attic or garage. Make your home your sanctuary. The less clutter you have, the more at peace you will feel. The happier you feel, the more relaxed your body will be, which means less stress and tension.

Be the buffalo! Buffalo hate storms and rain, like many animals; but most animals, when they sense a storm brewing, run in the opposite direction with the intention of outrunning the downpour. This technique doesn't work – the weather can and usually does move as fast as, if not faster than them. So running away from the rain can prolong the time they spend getting wet as the animals and the weather are moving at pretty much the same pace. Buffalo do the opposite: they hate storms so much that they run towards them. This makes the impact hard and fast, yes; but it also means it's over in as little as a few minutes.

Be brave and face life head-on like buffalo. When something doesn't go your way, or there is an awkward conversation to have, it's all too easy to avoid the person or situation. To sweep it under the rug into a festering 'not-going-there' pile. Unfortunately, it is still there, turning rancid. Ignoring the elephant in the room doesn't make it go away and your body knows this and will dutifully produce the stress hormones needed to get you out of or fight off the danger. This has a knock-on effect on the rest of the body, especially with long-term stress. Letting go or dealing with the problem (providing it's safe to do so) is the pathway to peace.

Problems rarely resolve themselves; more often than not, concerns ignored just escalate. An excellent example of this is an illness: all too often, people know they have a lump or some other issue but, rather than dealing with it, come up with a multitude of excuses not to, and so their condition just gets worse, or they just worry themselves (literally) sick about it.

Thankfully, of course, not all lumps or issues do escalate, but it's easy to get very stressed about things and bury your head in the sand when you could have got the all-clear or the necessary treatment if you had had the courage to seek help.

Write a list of everything you have been putting off, and tackle it – if it's concerning you, then it's depleting your energy and dragging you down.

Visualising

Visualising your favourite tranquil scene, whether that's a beach, a sunset, a mountain, a rolling field or anything else, can ground and relax you, stimulating the parasympathetic nervous system.

Take a moment to imagine a perfect tranquil place. See it clearly and zoom into every minute detail. How does it smell? What does it feel like? Is it warm or cool, bright or dark? What can you touch? Can you hear the sea, or cows mooing, perhaps rain or wind?

If visualising isn't the best way for you to use your imagination, focus instead on how your personal paradise makes you feel. Or find a picture of a place that is or looks like heaven to you and step into the scene. Give yourself the freedom to believe that you are in the picture and bring it to life. What would it feel like to be there?

As you do this, your mind focuses on these details rather than the stress you are experiencing. You will notice that you start to calm down.

Breathing

An old favourite. When you are stressed, your breathing tends to quicken and become shallow, coming from high up in the chest. Slowing, relaxing and deepening your breath is a great way to de-stress. Are you breathing from your diaphragm? You can check if you are doing so by placing your hands on your stomach. If you can feel your belly rising and falling, you are taking diaphragmatic breaths. This will drop you into your parasympathetic nervous system.

EFT (Emotional Freedom Technique)

Gently tap with two fingers on the points on the illustration below, twice in order. This will help release tension in the body and calm you down. It's a simple, easy and free technique to shift you back into rest and digest.

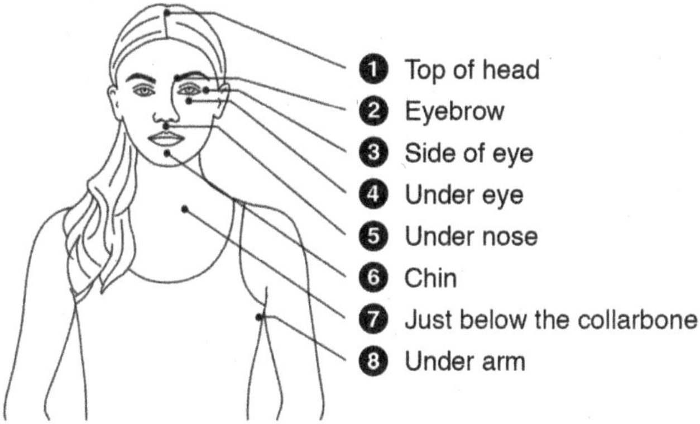

Remember, as humans, we need our trauma responses; they are vital for survival. However, we also deserve to feel energised, to flourish, to live in the moment and not have our energy wiped from us by other people, by events and by life's stresses. Think back to the seven-day log I suggested you keep earlier in the chapter. Can you continue keeping a log, every day, of how your energy feels? Write down how it is in the morning, at noon and at night. By working with it, along with all you have learned in this chapter, you will start to see a pattern. Notice when you are triggered and how you react. Can you adapt and be a little kinder to yourself? Are you feeling overwhelmed? Do you have clear boundaries? We will cover this more in later chapters. You will be able to do the work to regulate your nervous system and you will attract wonderful things that make you happy, fulfilled and add joy to your life.

1 How do I respond to trauma? Does my body do specific things? Do my shoulders tighten? Do I become anxious? Does my breathing become shallow? Can I think of situations when I've experienced them? Which ones? In response to what?

....

....

....

2 Have I taken on other people's stress and dramas recently? Has someone said something that I have found catty or hurtful? Were any of these dramas or

comments really about me? How can I not take these on going forwards?

....

....

....

3 Is there a hobby that I used to do and found nourishing, or would like to do?

....

....

....

4 I will, today, clear out this room/area/drawer in my house:

....

5 Do I experience moments of zen, calmness and peace? How frequently? What am I doing when I feel relaxed?
Some of the things that help me to relax are:

....

....

....

6 Do I have times when I feel that I am living harmoniously? How often? Some of those times are:

....

....

....

7 How do I like to exercise or move my body?

....

....

....

CHAPTER TWO

Social Media and Your Energy: The Good and the Bad, the Ugly and Beautiful

You may have noticed that social media immediately affects your energy and how you feel. Perhaps, after you have spent hours aimlessly scrolling through one of the social media platforms, you feel depressed or empty? If so, you are not alone. These platforms are designed to keep you coming back, day after day, hour after hour.

Advertisers want you to find their products and services through social media. Celebrities, individuals and corporations want you to keep returning to their pages and feeds to keep their public profile up. Have you ever looked to see how much time you spend online on your phone? The statistics can be scary!

In this chapter, I am going to help you become aware of the effects of social media, how it can drain your energy and change your mood in an instant – and, more importantly, what you can do to stop this from happening.

Every aspect of life seems to be becoming digital. While none of us can slow down technological advancements and digital developments, we can decide how much energy we give them, how often we invite this outside energy into our lives and how we manage the time we spend online.

ENERGY HACK

Turn on your phone's screen-time setting but don't check it for a week so you can see the natural pattern of where you are going and what you're spending time online doing. Then check it (you may be shocked!). In week two reduce your screen time by 10 per cent, and in week three reduce it by another 10 per cent. Within two weeks you will have gained more time, more energy and more mental clarity, just by spending less time online. Being aware of how you spend time and energy is critical in terms of creating the life you want to lead. This will ensure you thrive, are content and are constantly taking care of your own energy and how you spend it.

Did you know every time you get a like on Instagram or Facebook you receive a mini dopamine dose? Dopamine is a 'happy hormone', and it gives you a little buzz. Unfortunately for you – and by design – the hit is so tiny that you are far from sated. Instead, you want more and more, and this keeps you posting, always searching for a bigger hit. The more likes you get, the bigger the buzz – well, that is until you get used to however many hits you receive per post. Then you strive for more. As you become accustomed to the next level of hits and recognition, the buzz wears off, so you want a bigger buzz – and so it goes on.

This cycle of accruing social media likes and the dopamine rewards it gives you has parallels to a smoking addiction, insofar as you are never quite satisfied enough to take a break. With alcohol or drug abuse, after a big binge, most people choose to lay off the substance of choice for a while, or at least lower the dosage.

Some people have addiction problems with gambling. The inventors of social media cleverly took their inspiration from slot machines; it's easy to see the similarities. Slot machines have colourful lights and appealing sounds to give you a boost and entice you to sit there for hours, until your pockets are utterly devoid of funds. If you have ever been to Las Vegas, or even to your local pub with a slot machine, you will know exactly what I mean. In both situations, it's probably fair to say the house always wins.

There is no denying that social media is an integral part of modern-day culture, and that it can be fun and beneficial, but it comes without warnings or an instruction manual. As with everything we experience in life, I believe that moderation is key. Everything in moderation, including moderation! If you are disciplined with whom you follow and engage with, and limit your screen time, social media can be a massive asset to your life. On the other hand, it comes with a plethora of potential problems. Staring at your phone can be antisocial; you are less likely to be engaging with friends and loved ones, who are there physically in the room with you. You are also less likely to be partaking in nourishing pursuits.

Think of your energy system like a set of scales. Some things add value and others deplete you. Make sure you follow and engage with accounts that uplift you, and that you keep up with other things you love too. Balance your energetic scales.

It's very easy to tear people down and a lot harder to build a life you are proud of. People who haven't achieved their goals can get bitter and mean and take it out on others. It's unlikely you would approach a stranger in the street and start dissing them. We need to always remember that people say things online they would never say to each other's faces. Celebrities are a good example of this; even before social media came into existence, thanks to 'old media' like television, people felt connected to them and as if they knew them – and that they had a right to criticise them. The effect on strangers through a TV or cinema screen is astonishing. People find it easy to mistake the character for the actor. It's even common for actors to get jeered on the street when their character has misbehaved. We can now access celebs in a way never before seen. At the tap of a button, you can comment on a post or converse with someone you adore or abhor. It's easy to forget that, no matter what they (or their character) may have done, they have feelings too and negative comments are hurtful to anyone on the receiving end.

Then we have the pressures of comparison. 'Keeping up with the Joneses', an idiom originating from a 1913 comic strip (to which 'Keeping up with the Kardashians' is a modern nod). It means comparing yourself to peers and neighbours as a benchmark of what lifestyle and flash toys you 'should' have. If you don't have the latest clothes/car/watch/whatever, you start to feel inadequate. Comparing yourself to others just sets you up for failure. You can never be them; you need to focus on being the best you.

Anything you fixate upon will deplete your life-force energy: jealousy, resentment and envy are detrimental to your emotional and energetic self; being negative is actually exhausting! Your energy could be better spent on nourishing and productive pursuits. There are only so many hours in the day, and not much free time once you have accounted for work, travel, food prep and eating, family, chores, movement and sleep. Make the time that you do have count.

Happiness is an inside job; you need to build it yourself. It doesn't come from external pursuits.

We also have a coveting culture: we see someone's achievements without understanding the blood, sweat, tears and failures it took to get there, and this can make us feel resentful.

Social media can be a cesspit of envy. People borrow 'props', be they jets, cars or homes, and pretend they are living the high life. You can even rent a grounded private jet by the hour, take pictures on the runway and inside, pretending to be a passenger, then hop on an easyJet flight.

Remember – don't believe everything you see online. We only see the 'finished product', whether that be an individual, their beautiful home, their adorable children or perfectly behaved pets... You can be fairly sure that images and reels are carefully composed and doctored. Good lighting and posing make a world of difference, and then there is Photoshop and endless image-altering apps.

It's often easier to engage with people online than it is to speak to them in person. Live events can't be carefully curated to make you look good. This causes social anxiety in real-life situations. People are losing connection as well as social skills. It can be tempting to juggle mealtimes with devices when we're tired from a long day. Sometimes we are too busy with workloads or trying to keep control of our children to share our day with the people we are with. It's important to make time to connect to loved ones, whenever that is in your day.

Our social media culture has some very dark aspects indeed. If you look at social media regularly, you probably have a good idea of the posts, reels and stories that get the most likes and which TikTok videos go viral. Unfortunately, beautiful scenery and inspirational quotes rarely have the same impact as scantily clad people in holiday snaps. This realisation creates a vicious, unfulfilling cycle. Some social media is degrading and even pornographic. Unfortunately, showing flesh, or stupid and even dangerous behaviour, is one technique people use to increase engagement fast.

Virtual bullying has also played a considerable role in recent years. Caroline Flack's suicide, to give one example, was a terrible tragedy, and for many of us, I think, really brought home for the first time the impact that bullying and cyberslander can have.

Sadly, suicide and self-harm rates in children and young adults are steadily increasing. Horrifyingly, suicide is the second most common cause of death in young Americans. There is evidence to suggest that the increase in suicide is reflected in social media use. Fourteen to 21 per cent of young people now self-harm, and there is a correlation between those who self-harm and those who spend hours on their devices.[1]

Knowing all of this, you can now be more aware of the darker side of social media – the comparisons that aren't based in truth, the sheer amount of time that can be spent on the various platforms and how it can leave you feeling flat, empty and not good enough. The dent in your self-worth you feel after using social media.

As with all things, though, there are positives as well as negatives to social media. If you learn how to use it with awareness to enhance your energy, there can be wonderful benefits – among other things, it can motivate you, encourage gratitude and leave you feeling focused. You must be aware of how you are using it, why you are using it and the role it plays in your life, otherwise you are giving social media platforms an Access All Areas pass to drain your energy.

Social media platforms are just tools. As with any tool, how you use it determines if it is good or bad. A car can be a weapon or a vehicle to bring food to starving people or to deliver you to your destination. It's up to you to choose how you use your 'socials'. They may disconnect you from the people you are with, but they do make it easier to connect to people in faraway lands and forge friendships with people you would never have met in 'real life'. You may have more in common with a person halfway across the world than you do with your neighbour or own family.

Ideas can go viral in the blink of an eye; because of this, the development of the internet and the spread of wisdom has created an unfathomable speed of progress.

The Covid pandemic lockdowns were tough, but social media kept us connected. During that time we were not allowed to see people, to touch them or connect in person. Thank goodness we could still speak to loved ones over socials! If we hadn't been able to do that, I believe that despair, and even suicide rates, would have been far worse.

I, like many others, used my Oculus virtual-reality device to stay in touch with people during those long, dark nights of lockdown. At least there you could meet with friends and – virtually – share a drink, meal or adventure.

GETTING THE BEST OUT OF SOCIAL MEDIA

If you use social media well, it can be a great asset to your life and business. I want to teach you how you can get the very best out of the platforms you use – to ensure you feel positive, empowered and energetically full of life. Here are my top 10 tips for you to use to make sure the days of doom-scrolling and feeling energetically flat after using social media are in the past!

1. Be highly selective about whom you follow. Keep it positive – go for inspirational people and pages that make you laugh. Fun, beautiful and educational accounts that lift your spirits rather than darken your days. It's good to be well informed and know what's going on, but beware of falling down gloomy rabbit holes, spaces that deplete and upset you.

   Every interest you have will be accounted for on social media, and the algorithms are very sophisticated. Simply search for your favourite things and applicable accounts will appear on your feed. Social media can be a wonderful place to learn, grow and meet like-minded people.

   However, if you don't like the way someone is behaving, take a break from them. You can mute, silence and block accounts if they are damaging to your mental health. This goes for celebs and brands, as well as friends. If you feel someone is being creepy or is into something out of alignment with your values, just block them.

2. Choose peace over war by avoiding online confrontation. There is no need to get anxious by having arguments with random strangers or imaginary enemies. I'm sure that, at one time or another, most of us have engaged in heated debates on social media about politics, religion, people, etc. In my opinion the problem with heated debates, especially online, is that everyone is trying to prove their point rather than listen and learn. No one is searching for a middle way, new knowledge or compromise. They just want to be right. It's impossible and fruitless to battle against someone who is determined to be correct. The more you battle, the more exhausted you become. Online war is endless and depleting; rather annoyingly, no one ultimately wins. These sorts of rows often get aggressive and even personal. It's a negative, upsetting and depleting spiral sapping your energy; you could easily avoid all the upset, and conserve your energy, by scrolling past.
3. Remember, not everyone online is genuine – you could be fighting against a robot or a catfish (someone pretending to be someone else). My advice is to avoid online drama altogether: only go to war for things that truly matter and do it in the real world. Save your energy for things that spark joy and things you need to do.

4. It's easy to endlessly scroll through your feed and garner a plethora of random information. This has its merits when you have bountiful time; you can learn wondrous things and connect to amazing people. Mostly, though, you probably just want to know what your nearest and dearest are up to. If that's the case, rather than scrolling, go directly to your loved ones' accounts to see their updates. Click only on their pages and cut out the background noise. Or better yet, call them or arrange a meet-up. Also, make sure you have enough left in your tank for those closest to you.
5. Turn off your phone during meals, or at least don't look at your socials. Mealtimes are for connecting with loved ones. Spending your whole time scrolling is bad manners. Being distracted rather than present while you eat can cause you to overeat. A great example of this is when you go to the cinema: you are so engaged in the movie and the epic sound effects that you don't realise you have consumed a tub of popcorn larger than the average house cat! If you were sitting quietly without a screen, you might have eaten less. If you are overweight and want to lose some, simply being more aware of what you eat by being present and avoiding screens, be they big or small, during meals can go a long way to aid your weight-loss journey.
6. Meals with friends. If all of your friends are addicted

to their phones, you could play a game at dinner. Stack all the phones in the centre of the table. Whoever crumbles first and reaches for their mobile must buy everyone dinner, or at least a round of drinks. If you are playing in rounds, the person who crumbles has 30 seconds to check their phone and then re-stack.

The night could be very expensive, or it could be free, depending on your levels of personal discipline!

7. Turn off your phone when you go to bed. Having your phone on keeps you alert, anxious and sleeping lightly. Your phone flashing, beeping or, worse yet, ringing in the twilight hours will disturb your slumber. The less good-quality sleep you have, the faster you decay – yes, I mean age. So, get your Zs by having your phone off. If you have children or elderly parents, you may not want to turn off your phone in case there is an emergency call. If this is the case, consider getting a phone line installed in your bedroom that is exclusively reserved for loved ones in a pickle. Tell people to only contact you on that number in case of emergency.
8. If you are feeling hardcore, make a decision not to engage in social media after 8 p.m. That way, you can relax in the evening with a book or spend time with your family. The blue light emanating from your phone or telly is said to damage your sleep

cycle, so limiting screen time as you wind down is sensible. This is particularly helpful if you tend to argue with strangers online or get riled up while looking at your feed.

9. Detox. If you spend too much time online, take a few days off. You don't need to announce it to the world. Just take a break and see how you feel.
10. Plan your content, post it and leave. Even if you are using social media for work, you don't need to spend your whole day there. Wean your way off your phone. You could start by reducing your screen time by 15, 30 or 60 minutes a day, depending on your current usage. Alternatively, delete the apps and allocate 15-30 minutes at the beginning and end of your day to catch up with messages via your computer. In that way the apps aren't harassing you and you can still keep in touch. Or better yet, migrate your conversations to more communication-based platforms like WhatsApp or Telegram. See how you feel. Has your happiness increased with less phone time? If so, keep doing it; if not, keep doing it!

Use these tips for a more positive, focused social media experience.

Time is a great privilege and you get to decide how you use yours. Your time is too precious to simply hand over to large corporations and fall into advertising traps.

Remember – once you have the knowledge about how to protect your energy and focus, it becomes infectious. You don't want to look back on your time thinking you never achieved your full potential because you got distracted by modern-day technology. You want to look back and know you used technology to help you; you used it at the right time and in the right way.

The changes I have suggested you make are all quite small on their own but can have mighty results. Now that you have more knowledge, insight and confidence about ways to use social media, redirect your energy. Social media doesn't need to deplete you; it's just a tool. Make your online experience positive and uplifting by choosing to make it serve you and bolster your happiness.

Try allocating the time you would have spent online to something that makes you feel fulfilled, happy and positive. It's easy to spend your free time on your phone if you have nothing else to do, so find something else. Get outside, take up a hobby, spend time with friends, exercise, learn a new skill or set up a side hustle. The choice is yours; you decide how you spend your time, so spend it wisely.

1 How many social media platforms am I on? How much time do I spend on them in a day? A week?

....

....

....

2 Have I criticised celebrities or anyone else online? How would I feel if I received the comments I have posted or read them about myself?

....

....

....

3 Who do I think I need to keep up with? If I asked a friend, might they say there were things about me that they felt they should keep up with?

....

....

....

4 Who would I keep in touch with if I didn't have social media? How does that number of people compare to the numbers I follow and 'see' on social media?

....

....

....

5 What social event do I have coming up where I could leave my phone at home?

....

....

....

6 Feeds/topics I follow online that feed my energy positively are:

....

....

....

7 Three things I will spend an evening doing instead of being on my phone are:

....

....

....

CHAPTER THREE

Energetic Boundaries and Spiritual Hygiene

At times this chapter may make for uncomfortable reading. Setting and keeping boundaries, practising self-care and prioritising oneself are often some of the last things that we think about doing.

Well things are about to change! Always remember that you have the power and the right to define and set boundaries that protect your energy. I am going to give you the tools to start putting some serious energetic boundaries in place, coupled with, perhaps, a sobering look at your spiritual hygiene.

There is a reason why when you fly, the cabin crew tell you to put on your oxygen mask before helping others. If you are dead, you can't help anyone. The same goes for when you are depleted. Functioning with low energy and no headspace can be near impossible. You were born to function at 100 per cent. In this chapter I'm going to teach you how. These changes, tips and suggestions, as with all the advice I give you in this book, can have huge benefits for your quality of life, your energy and your outlook. Life moves at a fast pace and it's easy to forget to put yourself first. Your life may be so busy that, at the end of the day, you feel exhausted, pulled in a million different directions and have spread yourself too thin. Before I became aware of the amazing ways you can protect your energy, I was also feeling like this. The good news is it doesn't have to be this way. To achieve true, long-lasting change you must put one foot in front of the other, every single day. Change doesn't happen overnight and it's the consistent implementation of strong, energetic boundaries and good spiritual hygiene that I believe will have the biggest effect on your energy and how you feel.

I covered the effects of fight and flight mode in the first chapter, so you now know the devastating effect living in this state can have on your energy. It's also important to remember that when you are in survival mode, your world gets smaller. There is no space to create, flow, build and love; there is no generosity of spirit. You are just trying to make it through the day. You deplete your natural resources rather than cultivate new ones and expand. If you don't make time for your wellness, sickness will force you to rest. The truth is that self-care isn't selfish. Self-care is a necessity.

You may have experienced times when you have felt chronically stressed, overcommitted and exhausted. Moreover, did you know millions of workdays are lost annually due to stress? The crux is that stress is a killer, so minimising it is a no-brainer. You know now the effect that trauma can have on the mind, body and soul, and that stress can tear through your body and emotions, leaving you feeling exhausted and burnt out. Unfortunately, some people's self-worth is linked to how much they can do for others, with little to no thought or concern about how it affects them. A great example of this is what psychotherapists would refer to as the empathetic narcissist relationship, which is all too familiar, especially with those on the spiritual path. People on the spiritual path tend to be empaths; they can feel someone else suffering and want to help. Unfortunately, this kindness can be abused by people who lack empathy, namely narcissists. Narcissists are energetic vampires; they find it hard to create their own joy and happiness but seek emotional and energetic nourishment. The quality of the sustenance doesn't matter to them and they often leave the empath feeling drained.

ENERGY HACK

Keep a log of your everyday life. What you have done? Who you have seen? How did you feel before and after? Be observant as you go along and look back at the log after a week. You will likely be surprised at the results. You will soon start to notice the difference between people who leave you feel energised and people who leave you feeling drained. 'Radiators' will leave you feeling full of life, positive, full of energy and happy. 'Drainers' will literally drain your energy and leave you feeling negative, flat, empty and depleted of energy. Choose who you give your time to wisely!

Spiritual hygiene is a must. You wouldn't live in a filthy home, so why let your energy get gunky? Gunky energy, stress and overwhelm can lead to sickness, as well as to your body and mind running on empty with no clarity of thought or joie de vivre. Taking a proactive stance on how to stay sane in tough times is essential – and surprisingly simple. This chapter will explore what to do before, during and after uncomfortable encounters to help you put your best foot forward and shine, even in adversity.

WHAT TO DO WHEN YOU ARE OVERWHELMED

It's easy for things to mount up and for you to feel a sense of overwhelm. I have formulated 10 fast and actionable takeaways to protect your energy, stop overwhelm in its tracks and help you feel supported as you move forwards into a new chapter of high-vibrational living and thriving at 100 per cent every day!

1. **Ask for help.** Many people aren't great at asking for help – myself included; I can be a force of nature, so at times my ego doesn't like admitting weakness. Sound familiar? I'm better at asking for help for other people, which feels like less of an imposition. I will tell you what I tell my students, who are all powerhouses in their own right: how would you feel if your friend struggled and asked for help? Would you be annoyed at them for daring to ask, or would you want to help? Even if a stranger needed assistance, would you help them? Flip that and imagine you are the friend or the stranger. Give people the opportunity to help. Treat yourself with as much love, compassion and respect as you would a stranger or, better yet, your best friend.
2. **Don't expect people to read your mind.** If you are overloaded with work or family commitments, ask for help. I bet most of your colleagues would be happy to help if you were in a pickle. That is not to say that you

can regularly offload your work onto someone else; there needs to be some give and take. Think of your relationships like a bank. How much are you depositing, and how much are you withdrawing? Taking more than you contribute creates an imbalance and, potentially, resentment, not to mention the breakdown of relationships. People don't want to feel taken advantage of. When you have the opportunity to help, take it and deposit it into the friendship bank. When you are in credit, because you have been a great pal, you can ask for help without guilt. People aren't mind readers, though; you need to clearly communicate how you feel. While you may be energetically aware, able to read people's emotions and energy, a lot of people may not be.

3. **Select the right friends.** One of my favourite quotes is by William Gibson: 'Before you diagnose yourself with depression or low self-esteem, first make sure that you are not, in fact, just surrounded by assholes.' This is a great reminder for you to spend time with people who uplift you, who make you feel energised, full of gratitude, alive and in the moment, rather

than those who bring you down. If you spend time with negative people, you will feel rubbish, your energy will deplete and you will give them everything you have to try to lift them out of their funk.

You want to connect with people and form amazing friendships through joy, not misery. Talk about your joy, not your suffering. Energy goes where your intention flows, so the more you talk about your joys, the more joy will find you; and the more you discuss your woes, the more suffering will find you. Be careful with your words as your words create wishes; the more energy you put into worrying and moaning, the worse your life will become. Note down what you talk about with your friends and family and how it makes you feel. Who do you spend the most time with, and is it a positive or uplifting experience? The results may surprise you. You can easily fall into friendships that aren't balanced and built on mutual gossiping and moaning. It's easy to gossip about friends or even reality TV, but it's ultimately unfulfilling, and the time could be devoted instead to more productive or nourishing endeavours. Talk about your dreams, your plans, your loves, not what so-and-so did or said. Gossiping has a low vibe and depletes you. A little bit of light-hearted chat about the people you know may be okay, but I'd suggest working to cut down on gossiping overall. If this resonates with you, find comfort in the fact that you are aware of this now and can make a change and protect the wonderful life you have created and your own pure energy.

4. **Have fun!** One of the main reasons people lack energy is that they are not doing enough of what nourishes their soul. Most people are not following their passion or bliss; they are stuck in a rut. The wheel of 'Eat, Sleep, Work, Repeat' is soul-destroying. Add a little fun to the mix. What I'm about to say may sound strange to those of you who are down in the dumps, but hear me out: you can find joy in any task; you just need to look for it. When you commute to work, play your favourite music or, better yet, read a book on a subject you are interested in but have never taken the time to research. If you are driving, download an audiobook, and fill your time and your mind with its world and characters, or with learning. If there is a grotty person at work, let it be or kill them with kindness; don't let a miserable person win and steal your energy and joy. Revel in being happy in the face of adversity. Your happiness is down to you. You can choose your mood; it's all about attitude. Contentment is not about what happens externally but about how you react to adversity. Not every day will go your way; you can only consistently control your reaction, so choose joy over anger and peace over war.

5. **Do your best.** Even if you find your work dull, do your best. When you do your best, you feel accomplished, which boosts your happy hormones and your energy. You might not be where you want to be in life quite yet, but the journey is what life is all about. You are more likely to be promoted or get a new job when you do your best and have a positive outlook. If you want to succeed and earn the big bucks, do your best even in the menial tasks. It sets a precedent and a standard for what you feel is acceptable. People know they can rely on you and will pick you for more significant jobs. Never half-ass anything! What's the point? Commit fully to all endeavours, so if they don't work out you know it's not because of a lack of effort.
6. **Nip negative thoughts in the bud, as soon as you notice them.** Mental and emotional discipline are crucial for a happy and energetically full life. When something doesn't go your way, throwing the baby away with the bathwater is all too easy. If you were magically given £1,440 and lost a tenner, would you throw the other £1,430 in the bin? I hope not! Yet that's what you

do when you have a bad ten minutes and let that ruin the rest of your day. Don't let negative thoughts or low-vibe interactions drain your energy and mindset. Nip them in the bud and go back to thriving.

7. **Make time to dance!** Did you know that dancing boosts endorphins and promotes happiness? I love to dance as I cook or do housework. Dancing makes the mundane magical. It's common for people to dance less as they reach maturity; they no longer have time to attend gigs or concerts, as careers, commitments and family life take priority. Incorporate dance into your life; you could do a dance class, and boost your fitness as well as your joy. I love to work smarter, not harder, so dancing while ironing or cooking is ideal – two birds, one stone. Inject more energy into your day by being physically active. Choose movements you enjoy. The best part is you don't have to spend money on going to a gym – dancing is free and you can do it anywhere!
8. **Have a sense of purpose.** Self-worth is intertwined with work and productivity. You wither away if you don't have a reason to get up in the morning and a sense of purpose. You can end up feeling so flat and listless that the thought of doing even the most basic tasks feels overwhelming. Service is linked to happiness. When you help others, you feel good about yourself. Volunteer to help a charity; help others out and watch your happiness skyrocket.

9. **Create and build.** When you make something with your hands – paint, sculpt or even put together a piece of flat-pack furniture – you engage the physical along with the mental. It's common for people with office jobs to rarely use their hands and minds together to create. It's nourishing to do so and is also a great way to replenish your energy; it calms your mind, as tasks like sculpting, pottery or building furniture can often be intricate and require a lot of focus.
10. **Get a hobby.** Work out what you like to do and spend more time doing it! If you can get outside the house to do it and have some 'me' time while you do, all the better. The problem with having a hobby at home is that there is always work to do – laundry, gardening, not to mention people vying for your attention. Attend an art or gym class. Go swimming or do whatever you love out in the world, making sure to leave the building. It will rejuvenate and reset you. By doing what you love you will feel alive, joyous and full of energy, ready to thrive and take on the rest of the day.

Once you have created an inspiring and purposeful life, you will have more life force to take on challenges. When you have more life force, it's easier to say no to things that don't bring you joy. As I've said before, knowing you are in control of your life and your energy becomes infectious – you want to do more of what makes you feel alive and wonderful. If you are too tired or feeling energetically empty, you might find yourself saying yes to things to 'keep the peace' or to avoid an argument. Seeing it as the lesser of two evils, you go along with things, believing this will deplete you less. As you start to feel safer in your own skin by implementing some of these fast and actionable tips, I recommend making the conscious choice of deciding that if it's not a HELL, YES! it's a NO! Going through with unwanted commitments, can lead to resentment or feeling overwhelmed. If you don't fulfil your obligations, you let people down, which can damage relationships. Don't commit to anything that doesn't bring you happiness or joy or replenish your energy source. Try this for a week and watch the transformation begin.

We have now covered how to combat overwhelm and avoid it draining you, leaving you empty. Next, we need to address what to do when you find yourself somewhere that you don't want to be. I believe that by introducing stronger energetic boundaries and spiritual hygiene, these moments will start to diminish. I want to arm you with all the information you may need in case these situations do arise because I understand that change takes time. You will become more aware of situations and environments that leave you feeling alienated and devoid of energy. If you find yourself somewhere, you don't want to be, then these are my top tips for how to handle the situation. Remember, if you continue to repeat the pattern of being in places you don't want to be or ending up in situations you'd rather not be in, it will become a choice. You are in control, you have the power to edit your life in real time and to decide who gets a place in it. Never forget, you've got this and you are the captain of your own ship; you are the boss, your energy is up to you.

Here are my top 10 tips for what to do before the event if you've ended up agreeing to go somewhere you don't want to be.

1. **If it's not a HELL, YES, it's a NO!** Remember, you are in control, you deserve a life full of HELL-YES moments! Your life will become a beautiful montage of high-vibrational experiences that leave you feeling energetically charged and overflowing with gratitude if you follow this mantra. Do not underestimate the simplicity; it's gold dust and they are words to live by.

2. **Protect yourself energetically before you enter a space.** Just before you leave home, sit quietly with your eyes closed and visualise a marble-sized ball of brilliant white light in the centre of your chest. If it starts dull or grey, give yourself a few moments to irradiate the marble, until it becomes blindingly bright. Once the marble is radiant, you can begin to

expand it, gradually making it more prominent. The marble becomes a golf ball, the golf ball becomes a tennis ball and the tennis ball becomes a beach ball. Incrementally increase the size of the ball, ensuring it stays luminous white, verging on ice blue. The beach ball becomes a gym ball, and the gym ball expands beyond the size of you with your arms and legs outstretched. Sit peacefully in the shiny ball of white light for a few minutes; the light will pump you up, so you are better able to cope with your environment, and things that would usually irritate you bounce off. Travel to where you are going. If you are a passenger, you can pay attention to your forcefield and ensure it is still radiant, enveloping your whole body as you go. Before you enter your engagement, pump up your shield. If you find yourself getting triggered, excuse yourself to the bathroom and take a moment to fortify your barrier before returning. This technique can be used whenever you like; you don't need to save it for taxing times. You could use it as a daily practice – when you take a shower, or sit for a few moments before you leave home, or at any point in your day, especially if you are approaching something that may cause you anxiety. The more you do it, the easier it will become. Definitely use it before entering a social war-zone!

3. **During the rendezvous, take a break.** If you find yourself boiling with anger, step away, and take a

break. If you can go outside and have some alone time, do so. Even better, ground yourself by taking off your shoes and socks and standing barefoot on a natural surface, such as grass or sand. Concrete won't help.

4. **Remember to breathe.** If anxiety strikes, breathing is your buddy. Stale air gets trapped in your lungs and needs to be replaced with fresh air. The out-breath is vital. Breathe all the air out of your lungs, until there is none left, then breathe in until you feel full, after which do a slow exhale for as long as you can. If you are new to focused breathwork, start with 7–10 seconds; if this is easy for you, extend your breath. Follow it with a slow inhale for the same time. Do this for a minute. This should calm your nerves.

   Why not try the 5, 4 ,3, 2, 1 method to bring you back into the present moment? List five things you can see, four things you can touch, three things you can hear, two things you can smell, and one thing you can taste. This will help ground your energy, helping you to focus. It will calm your nervous system, regulate your breathing and still your thought patterns.

5. **It's not you; it's them.** If someone is being difficult, it says more about them than you. Happy people are kind to others; miserable people moan and are rude. If someone is difficult, realise it's probably because they are unhappy. Reacting to someone's snide comments will likely escalate the drama, so just let it be. Sometimes you just need to suck it up, buttercup! Note that this is

only for minor infringements. Real abuse needs to be dealt with in a safe, controlled manner.

6. **Work on yourself.** You attract what you focus on and what is in your energetic field. If you have been betrayed and not worked through it or come to peace with it, you will continue to invite betrayal; the key is to stop ordering things you don't want from the universe. If you don't release trauma, you keep reordering suffering. (More on this when I explain the dark side of the law of attraction.) If you get triggered, make a mental or written note of what happened, and work through it later. It's possible to get to the stage when firstly, people rarely say or do the upsetting things and, secondly, if they do, you don't really care.
7. **Take your time.** It's easy to get flustered when you are stressed. Being flustered may make you clumsy, flappy and prone to mistakes. Don't allow others to rush you; do things at your pace. Planning really helps with this.
8. **Limit your alcohol consumption.** This will help protect your auric field (your energetic force field). A strong aura allows you to be grounded, centred and focused, however when you drink, your auric field weakens, and the daemons start their party. The daemons I'm referring to are self-deprecating thoughts and paranoia. You may begin to see and hear things that aren't accurate. Alcohol can

escalate anxiety and brain chatter. Some people can handle alcohol; they can take it or leave it. They don't drink excessively, have a buzzy time and are just bouncier. Others, however, may not know when to stop, get 'the fear' the following day or become a 'mean drunk'. If you are not at your best when you have had a tipple, you may want to give it a miss.

There are quite a few new drinks on the market these days that are great for non-drinkers and for people who want to cut down, but still enjoy the 'buzz'. I have recently discovered one of these alcohol alternatives, Sentia. It is designed to activate the GABA receptors in your brain in the same way that alcohol does. It is a non-alcoholic 'spirit' made of botanical ingredients, and it claims to provide you with a happy, silly buzz – but only up to a point; you stay at the sociable sweet spot of being a giggly fun drunk, with no hangover and it's low-calorie! They say it gives you what you want from alcohol without the alcohol, so is perfect for uncomfortable encounters. This is great for when you do feel that you want the buzz of alcohol but don't want to take it too far. Seedlip is another sophisticated non-alcoholic drink, made from beautiful botanicals, to be drunk with tonic or other mixers. Three Spirits have a range of alcohol-free spirits with added benefits: one claims to be energising and another is a 'nightcap' for when you are ready to wind down. These drinks are all low in calories and sugar. As such, they are a very interesting adult addition to the standard range of soft drinks. Why not give them a try?

9. **Just say 'NO'.** If you feel uncomfortable, you can say no to activities – yes, even if the suggestion comes from your mother-in-law or boss.
10. **Planning.** Planning alleviates stress. Make sure to arrive at appointments and social arrangements on time; being late adds an unnecessary layer of stress. Limit your time at events you would rather not be at, giving fair warning to the organisers.

Congratulations, you made it through an awkward event! Now it's time to cleanse and reset. As you know, life can sometimes throw you a curveball and, with the best intentions in the world, you may still have some problematic encounters that catch you off guard and drain your energy. The good news is you are going to learn how to reset your mind and energy after kerfuffles. You are human and these things will happen. The power is in learning from each encounter and reinforcing your energetic boundaries so much so that it becomes second nature to you.

Here are my top 10 tips and pieces of advice for you to protect your energy and reset after an awkward encounter. You don't need to do all of them but I would advise you try them all at least once to see which ones resonate with your own energetic fields and feelings.

1. **Cleanse.** If you are feeling like you've picked up negative energy from somewhere or someone, the best thing to do is cleanse as soon as you can. Taking a shower or bath is one of the most underrated cleansing rituals. You can literally take the day off and wash your troubles away. You always feel better and refreshed when you are clean. If you would rather a bath, use some Epsom salts. Epsom salts have extensive healing properties; they ground you and dissolve negative energy, as well as relaxing muscles and the mind. You could also add essential oils to your bath. There are so many to choose from: I love rosemary to increase cognitive function and lower stress; ylang ylang is perfect for stress and overall support; cedarwood is anti-inflammatory with earthy notes and lemon is refreshing and energising. Lavender is relaxing, while tea tree is a decongestant. I tend to buy a multipack and use what feels right on the day. Just be sure not to use essential oils directly on the skin.

2. **Smudging.** An uncomfortable exchange in your home may have left some bad juju. Energy has substance, which is why you can feel anger in the air after a fight and why your home feels lighter after you have a clear-out. Smudging your house to cleanse the air after an argument, after you have felt upset or uncomfortable is fast, easy and simple. Amazingly, smudging also cleans the air and is said to kill up to 94 per cent of airborne bacteria.[1] I would suggest you smudge using palo santo (please ensure it is ethically sourced) or sage whenever you feel the air is a little stale and in need of a purge and reset; both are widely available and easy to use. Light the sage stick or palo santo and let it slowly smoke. It should not have a flame, so if this happens, gently blow it out and allow it to start smoking with no flame. Always make sure you have a glass of water nearby when you are performing this in your house in case you need to extinguish the smoke quickly. Open the windows in all the rooms and smudge in a clockwise motion. The negative energy that has collected in the house will start to leave through the windows.
3. **Reflection.** Take some time to reflect on events in your life. How did an encounter go? How did you handle adversity? Were you triggered, or did you ride the wave of drama like a pro? Journaling is helpful here, as you can monitor your progress; it's

wonderful looking back months or even years later to see how far you have come.

4. **Talk it out.** Be mindful of who you discuss your grievances with. If your issue is with your mother-in-law, your spouse might not be the best person to talk to. Discuss problems with friends who have a sympathetic ear or those who are solution-orientated. Avoid friends who get you riled up and escalate your frustration; getting more upset serves no purpose.
5. **Don't beat yourself up. It's okay!** If you did have a meltdown, it just means there is room for improvement. Pity parties and endlessly lamenting about behaviour are a total waste of time. Beyoncé has a brilliant attitude to adversity. She gives herself one day to feel sorry for herself. Twenty-four hours to feel it; she allows herself to swim in her emotions, bathe in sorrow and anger. The following day, she gets up and moves on, no longer dwelling on the drama.
6. **Do the work.** None of us are perfect. We all mess up from time to time. Look for progress, not perfection. Now you have had time to reflect on what went wrong, you can work to neutralise your triggers and minimise any drama in your next encounter. Sit with what happened and work on forgiving all parties concerned. Distance yourself from memory. You could get yourself in a lovey-dovey, gooey state by reminiscing about a perfect day, person or pet.

Then think of your trauma; the high-vibe memory will help to neutralise the low-vibe one.

7. **Visualise scenes a) Before they happen** – If you know you need to have a difficult conversation, plan it. Prepare for all the directions it could go in and have a solution to every eventuality. The more you plan and prepare for uncomfortable situations, the better you will handle them in the moment. **b) After the fact** – Play out troubling scenes in your mind and conclude them favourably instead. View the scenes in their entirety rather than cherry-picking. Notice when conversations went awry and correct them.
8. **Get into nature**. You may have noticed that I regularly recommend getting into nature and grounding. That's because it is a superb way to quieten the mind chatter and relax the body. A simple walk in the woods or park will do. If you can get to the sea or another body of water, all the better. Paddling or swimming is better yet. Absorb as many of the water's negatively charged ions as possible; it will help you connect back to yourself and relax.
9. **Get your body moving.** Exercise is the perfect way to de-stress. Trauma stagnates, so moving really helps. Playing tennis and imagining the ball to be someone's head is an option! Or simply try running or lifting weights. Do an exercise you are fully present with; a strenuous one is ideal – one that gives you no time to think.

10. **Words to live by.** I love these little maxims; they are simple, effective and geared towards ensuring that you energetically cleanse yourself, reset and live more in the moment. Here they are:

    If you feel like everyone hates you, take a nap.
    If you feel like you hate yourself, take a shower.
    If you feel like you hate everyone, eat.

The advice and tips in this chapter are truly life-changing. Following these simple spiritual hygiene practices and setting clear boundaries will lead you to happiness. It will also help to reinforce your personal power; you are magical! Remember, you are in control of your own energy and life. You decide what you consume in terms of food, energy and interactions.

The buck stops with you – which is truly liberating. As simple as it sounds, if you don't like an aspect of your life or if, perhaps, my words have illuminated issues you have avoided, now's the time to start making small changes and stepping into your power. Become sovereign: remember, the only thing you can control is your response. Don't get swept up in drama; choose peace. You have one life – it is precious and it is driven by your energy: what you put in determines what you get out. You decide who comes into your life, you give space to them and you grant them a place at the table and in your life. Are you ready to start editing who has access? It's time to tune into who is a radiator or a drainer in your life. You've got this!

1 Who in my life is a radiator? Who is a drainer?

....

....

2 This week I will notice my negative thoughts and nip them in the bud. Some of them are:

....

....

3 Have I had any hell-yes moments this week?

....

4 What is one thing I can ask for help with this week?

....

....

5 Three things that are my passion or bliss:

....

....

6 Three songs I love to dance to:

....

....

CHAPTER FOUR

Gut Health, Happiness, Authenticity and Truth

For aeons, society has looked at the mind, body and soul as separate entities – treating them in an isolated way, compartmentalising wellness.

There are different doctors to treat the heart, the lungs, the reproductive system, the brain and so on. This approach goes against the fact that bodies are one. You are incredible and unique. If we think of people as broken up into sections, and isolate key organs or bodily systems, we can never live to our true energetically charged potential. The key is to look at the body holistically and work out what underpins a variety of ailments. In this chapter I'm going to teach you about happiness, authenticity, truth – and gut health! It may sound strange initially to discuss all these areas within the same chapter, but you will soon understand how they are intrinsically linked.

To have a deeper understanding of this area you need to start with your gut health.

Have you ever had a 'gut feeling', or butterflies in your stomach? These sensations demonstrate that your gut and your brain are connected. The communication system between them is called the gut–brain axis. These two organs are connected. You have almost 100 billion neurons, or nerve cells, in your brain.[1] They carry chemical and electrical signals helping you coordinate your functions in life. Neurons can also be found in your central nervous system, and sensory neurons are in your eyes and ears. Amazingly, your gut contains around 500 million neurons. They are connected to your brain via your nervous system. There are many ongoing studies and research into the gut–brain axis and the potentially huge influence it has on our health and energy. It's only in recent years that scientists have started to better understand the gut–brain axis and its impact – not only on physical and digestive issues such as IBS (irritable bowel syndrome), but also on mental-health conditions such as depression and anxiety.

Protecting your energy is crucial; it's important to be mindful of who and what you are giving your attention to. It's important to also carefully consider what you are putting into and taking out of your body.

What are you using as your fuel? Are you making sure you have enough energy in your tank to thrive every day?

Holistically viewing your body means you see it as one, free-flowing energetic system. When a single part is out of sync or unsettled, there are knock-on effects resulting in depleted energy.

If communication along your axis deteriorates, your physical and mental health may be compromised. Gut–brain communication happens via the vagus nerve, which is the biggest nerve in your body.

There are several additional pathways that are involved in the complex functioning of the gut–brain axis. This area of science is vast, and I urge you to continue doing more research into it; not only because it will help improve your life but because it really is fascinating. My aim is to give you a snapshot of this area so you can see the direct link between your emotional and physical health. The happier you are, the better your physical health will be. It's time to start your journey into health, to curate a bespoke approach specifically for you.

The complex functioning of the gut–brain axis includes communication through various chemical messengers, the endocrine (hormone) system, gut hormones and neurotransmitters. Many of these neurotransmitters and hormones are made in the gut, such as GABA (gamma aminobutyric acid), dopamine and serotonin. Carbohydrate fermentation produces by-products such as short chain fatty acids (SCFAs). To put it simply – what is happening in the gut can directly influence your brain function and behaviour.

By altering the types of bacteria in your gut, it may be possible to improve your brain health. Certain foods benefit your gut health and gut–brain axis. They include Omega-3 fatty acids, fermented foods, probiotics and other polyphenol-rich foods. Animal fats are important for cognitive function; I love bulletproof coffee, which contains coconut oil and butter. I also cook with ghee (clarified butter), as it doesn't degrade, even at high temperatures. For me, animal fats are vital; without them my critical thinking is dramatically compromised. I encourage you to play. To try different diets and tips from this book and work out what makes you feel healthy and happy.

I am fascinated by the subject of gut health for a multitude of reasons. Believe it or not, your gut microbiome (the community of microorganisms living in all our guts) is one of the foundations of health. In simple terms, good gut health occurs when you balance the good (helpful) and the bad (potentially harmful) bacteria and yeast in your digestive system.

Your body is the most incredible home you will ever own and live in. It is yours to nurture, nourish and care for. To put it simply, you have the option to live in a palace or a rubbish bin; you can choose to live in a healthy, well-cared-for and well-nourished body or to self-sabotage and deny your body the nutrients, self-love and energy fuel that it so desperately craves.

Self-love and energy optimisation can be practised in a vast array of ways. You show yourself love or neglect daily in the way you care for yourself. Your relationship with your mind, body and soul is the most important one you will ever have. I have dedicated my life to dissolving emotional trauma and dis-ease and have successfully helped to heal tens of thousands of people, transforming their lives. You have a responsibility to care for your own health, and to become educated on how to live with mind and body coherence.

Your gut is where the body digests and absorbs nutrients from the food you eat, giving you the energy to perform bodily tasks and functions. Your vitality and life force primarily come from what you consume. Have you noticed that when you eat fast food, after the initial energy spike and endorphin rush, you soon feel sluggish, bloated and even guilty about what you have put into your body? Fast food contains a multitude of horrible chemicals, added all along the process from farm to table. Eat organic, if at all possible; it has significantly higher nutritional value;[2] or better yet, if you have access to a garden, allotment or any patch of ground, grow your own!

Moreover, think of how you feel after eating a healthy, nutritious meal. There are, of course, many ways to eat. I recommend experimenting with different diets and seeing how you feel. If you are consistently sluggish after eating, change things up. I have played with a lot of diets in my time. The one that works best for me is high in animal fats and protein and low in carbs. A good intake of fats and protein makes you feel fuller for longer. Your blood sugar is more consistent without an immediate spike.[3] You are more productive with sustained energy. I also eat virtually no processed foods; the less processing our food has gone through, the better.

The body is truly magnificent. Did you know that 90 per cent of the absorption of vitamins and minerals happens in the small intestine? It's your engine. If you eat food with low nutritional value, you won't have the fuel you need to be productive.

A good diet is essential; but it is a little more complicated than that. It's not solely about the foods you eat. I regularly help people with poorly functioning small intestines. Some of them are on the best diets imaginable but are still fatigued – it's all dependent on how well their small intestine operates. If your small intestine is operating at 10 per cent of its optimum, even if you solely dine on ambrosia and nectar (the food of the gods), you will only be getting 10 per cent of amazing. Conversely, if your small intestine is working at 100 per cent and you primarily ingest fast food, you will be getting 100 per cent of the sparse nutrients, so you may have more energy and life force than the person who was eating more nutrient-rich food. It's not fair, but it's true. You can tap into bountiful energy, if you start making small, incremental and consistent changes. However, you cannot function at your best and achieve your full potential if you're running on empty. Running on empty means you will have low energy, and struggle with clarity and focus. When I say empty, I am talking about spiritually empty, emotionally empty and physically empty; these elements require energy, fuel and consistency to help you live a happy and fulfilled life.

Do you want to be living at 25 per cent capacity or lower? Or do you want to achieve more than you ever thought possible?

Gut balance affects our overall energy in all kinds of ways. Serotonin, a neurotransmitter associated with sleep and mood is produced in the intestines. This means that your digestive system plays a key role in your happiness. Microbiome disruptions can, therefore, directly impact restful sleep, plus your next day's energy and enthusiasm.

When it comes to your wellness and your health, remember that all-or-nothing approaches tend to be unsustainable. As you do more of your own research into digestive health, be open to ideas, and experiment. We are all different – there is no one-size-fits-all formula. Overhauling your diet and gut health overnight is unlikely to work; it is a long-term lifestyle change. You can start straight away by taking simple steps to move in the right direction. Experiment and find what works for you.

Some people find starting their morning with a matcha tea and a protein-filled breakfast provides them with energy until lunchtime. Others may choose a coffee and fruit salad. I fast until lunchtime; fasting actually gives me more energy. This may sound counterintuitive; however, it works for me. I know it's not always easy or possible to consistently eat organic or seasonally, but there is another way of eating I highly recommend. I'm pro-fatty meats and fruits. Natural fats are essential for cognitive function, and fruit is generally considered a good, healthy choice. As ever, though, use your own discretion and see what works for you.

ENERGY HACK

For one week I want you to drink only good water, be it filtered or bottled, and stick to eating whole foods. Include good-quality meat or other natural fats and proteins, with a variety of fruit and vegetables. Avoid processed food and white carbs. Eat food made with love at home. After the first few days of initially missing sugar, coffee, alcohol, whatever your usual 'things' are, you will start to feel amazing, your clarity of mind will sharpen and your energy levels will flourish.

Here are my top 10 tips to help you improve your energy:

1. **Get enough sleep.** When I say sleep, I don't mean dozing in front of the TV. It seems that a lot of people are sleep-deprived, so if you need a power-nap, then lie down and take it. As long as it doesn't compromise your sleep at night. You need a proper, restful night-time slumber that enables your cells to renew, your body to recharge and your physical maintenance to develop. Proper rest means you are able to replenish your energy for the next day, helping you to achieve your full potential. If you are exhausted but struggling to sleep, think about how you are spending the last two hours before bed. I'm going to hazard a guess that you may be scrolling through social media, perhaps watching TV, shopping online or reading news on your phone. Stimulation and screen time before bed is disruptive to sleep. It's time to take things old-school. Try a phone ban in the house from 8 p.m., or, at the very least, get blue-light-blocking glasses and screen protectors for your phone. An hour before you want to sleep, take a bath to unwind and light some

candles. Face and hair masks designed for sleep are great too.

2. **Journal your day.** The good, the not-so-good and everything in between. End the day on a high with three things you are grateful for. Once you've finished journaling, read a chapter of a book.
3. **Check your bedtime.** According to traditional Chinese medicine, the most important time to be asleep is between 11 p.m. and 1 a.m; the theory is that this is when your body does most of its rejuvenating.

A general rule of thumb could be to simply aim to go to sleep at 9 p.m or 10 p.m and wake when it's light. This one makes a huge difference to me and those I have recommended it to. Play around with different bedtimes and see how you feel. Start by trying to get to get to bed for 10 p.m and lights out by 10.30 p.m latest for a few weeks and see if you have more energy? I also like to go to bed early (mostly) and get up early, as I tend to be more productive in the morning. I do realise that this doesn't work for everyone. If you decide to rise and slumber with the sun, it's important to understand that you tend to need less sleep in summer. This has to do with the sun being the ultimate electron donor (more on this in the Body Voltage and Energy Cultivation chapter).

4. **Meditation.** It's a great thing to do before sleep. Meditation gets a bit of a Marmite response: people love it or hate it. It resonates with some people from the start. Others find it tough or think they can't do it.

   Meditation can feel overwhelming or off-putting, but I'm here to tell you that you can do it. By committing to this free and profound exercise, I believe that you can and will change your life for the better. If you find meditating tough, try a few different approaches and see what works for you. You could try an acupuncture mat. Lie on it in the evening while listening to some relaxing music (if you find the mat too uncomfortable, you could put a towel over it until you get used to it.) Acupuncture mats stimulate energy flow in the body and can be found online for around £20.

5. **Experiment with music.** What do you like to listen to for relaxation? You could try nature sounds, rain or 'spa' music? You may want to stay away from music with lyrics, unless it's a guided meditation, as words can bring you out of meditation.

   Many parents use white noise to help their babies sleep; rain is nature's own white noise and is proven to help overstimulated and overactive minds.[4] The repetitive, predictable and simple sound allows overstimulated brains to slip into light meditation. The mind becomes accustomed to the rhythmic and repetitive sound of rain fast – your brain is primed to be sympathetic to it.

6. **Stress levels.** These need to be lowered! Chronically high levels of stress are hard on your whole body. While I know that reducing stress is easier said than done, remind yourself that you are in control of your energy and life and, as such, must maintain, contain and protect your energy. How much of your day do you enjoy? I don't mean how much of your day do you tolerate; I mean how much do you really spend having fun – or even at peace? How much of the day do you feel you're thriving and not just going through the motions? Do you feel blessed? Do you feel grateful and excited by the life you're living or do you feel drained, depressed and stuck in Groundhog Day? Perhaps you feel somewhere in the middle, whereby you do things you like but overcommit to activities and engagements/friends that cause tension.
7. **Eat slowly.** This may sound overly simple, but how often do you truly eat in the moment and in a mindful way? We are all guilty sometimes of eating lunch on the go, grabbing something fast. Instead, try having a mindful lunch, eating presently and slowly. It will also ease the digestive process – making it kinder and easier on your body. Digestion starts in the mouth, so the more you chew, the easier it is on

your digestive system. It's all too common to wolf down a meal and move on to the next task, but I encourage you to savour the flavour and all the tastes and textures. If you are eating at home in the evening, do you really need the TV on for every single meal? It's easy to get caught up in what's happening on the screen and not pay attention to your food.

8. **Hygge.** The word 'hygge' (it appears in both Danish and Norwegian) describes a mood of cosiness and 'comfortable conviviality' – feelings of wellness and contentment. This approach is about simplicity, about being kind and nourishing to oneself and others. It's about incorporating cosy things like hot drinks, candles, cushions, etc. Each small act of self-love is enriching – anything that makes you smile is worth including in your day.

9. **Walk to create energy.** You could go for a walk on your lunch break, getting some steps in and taking in all your surroundings. If you are fortunate enough to work near a park or somewhere else in the great outdoors, bathe in nature over lunch. If you work in a busy city, what life is there to witness

and watch? Be present and appreciate your surroundings. Find your space and take your time. When life is busy, it can be very hard not to feel overwhelmed – we live in a modern-day world that is demanding. You do not need to participate in the rat race 24 hours a day. Unplugging yourself for 30 minutes will boost your energy much more than scoffing lunch in front of your computer and attending to even more emails.

10. **Drink up.** Good health relies heavily on hydration. It's worth knowing that around 60 per cent of your body is water, although this does vary according to gender and age. The function of water, hydration and their importance to your body and energy levels is mind-blowing. Water is the primary building block of cells. It acts as an insulator, regulating internal body temperature. When you drink plenty of water you repair, you flourish and you thrive. Make sure that you are drinking good-quality filtered or bottled water. It's easy to forget to drink enough; if that's the case for you, you could buy a water bottle with times on it to encourage you to drink a certain amount by a particular time. If you get sick of the taste of water try adding some lemon, mint or cucumber, like they do in upmarket spas.
11. **Meal planning.** Are you planning healthy meals to make before you go shopping? Avoid falling into the supermarket trap of buying unhealthy things

you don't need! Set aside 15 minutes each week to create a meal plan – how many natural foods packed with vitamins and minerals can you feed yourself to help fuel your body? Experiment with meat and fish or other whole food proteins and fats. Vary your fresh fruits and vegetables. Don't get stuck on one diet or another; even if you have eaten one way for a long time, try something new and see how you feel. Experiment in the kitchen, learn new recipes and enjoy your journey to better health and vitality!

ENERGY HACK

Have a 'Stress Pot' by your desk or somewhere else in your home to help bring awareness to your stress. Every time you feel a rush of stress that negatively impacts your energy, write it down with the time and the date and pop the note in the stress pot. At the end of the week, look at the results. They are likely to reveal a huge amount of repetition with heavily ingrained patterns showing up. Once you see the patterns, you can start to change them and make proactive choices to eliminate recurring stress in your life. You could keep the notes and refer back to them to monitor your progress. As you illuminate and eradicate your stress, your body and mind will begin to operate in a calmer state, and your energy will recover, rejuvenating your life force.

Now you have some insights and advice regarding how to improve your health and energy, you have a good foundation to naturally boost your serotonin, your energy supply and your mood.

I want to ask you a few questions:

Are you happy? Are you living in the moment? Are you content with your life? With how you feel and with what you have achieved? Or do you feel you could be happier but don't know how to get there? If so, fear not – I've got you. I am going to teach you some secrets to happiness that will benefit you – energetically, spiritually and physically.

The Harvard Study of Happiness is an amazing piece of research that began in 1938 and is still running, making it one of the longest of its kind.[5] It originally asked 724 men about their home lives, health and experiences. Sixty of the original men are still alive and participating, most of them in their nineties; the experiment now includes over 2,000 of their children, grandchildren and great-grandchildren.

At the start, the study took two groups of young men. The first were in their second year at the prestigious

Harvard University, the second were from some of the poorest Boston neighbourhoods, many from homes without hot or cold running water. Some became lawyers, some doctors; there were builders, bricklayers, even a US president. Some climbed from the bottom to the top in terms of their social standing and wealth, some went the other way. The study involves sending participants questions about their lives, in-person interviews and consultations with their friends and families. Their medical records are reviewed, and they have brain scans and all sorts of other medical checks. The less privileged men would regularly ask, 'Why do you keep wanting to study me? My life just isn't that interesting.' The Harvard men never asked that question. I find this an interesting side note; it just shows they are very different men.

What the study has learned and continues to find is that happiness has nothing to do with wealth, fame or working harder. Rather, the principal point researchers have taken away is: 'Good relationships keep us happier and healthier, period.'

There are three main lessons that can be taken from this study to help you improve your happiness and your positive energy. The first is social connections. Social connections are brilliant for us. It's been said that loneliness kills. The more socially connected to family and community we are, the happier and healthier we will be. Isolation means we are less content and our health declines earlier. Brain function decays sooner, and we live shorter lives than people who are less lonely.

Remember, it's not the number of friends you have or if you are in a committed relationship – rather it's the quality of close relationships that matters. As we saw in the energetic boundaries chapter, it's important that you don't invite friends into your life for the wrong reasons or simply to fill time. Friendships and relationships need to be energetically matched.

The Harvard Study of Happiness has looked at people in their fifties to predict who among them would be the healthiest octogenarians. It isn't middle-aged cholesterol that has the biggest effect, nor is it diet and exercise. It's how satisfied people are in their relationships in their fifties. By relationships they (and I) don't just mean marriage; it's about loving and being loved, having close friends and family. The study found that having close, loving ties has the single greatest effect on health into our eighties! People who were in unhappy relationships had their pain amplified by their emotional despair.

Good relationships don't just protect our bodies, they also protect our brains and feed into our own personal energy. If we are in our eighties and feel like we can count on our partners and loved ones in times of need our memories stay sharper for longer. If, however, we are alone or don't feel we can count on our partners, earlier memory decline is experienced. Some of the octogenarians in the Harvard study reported that they 'bicker day in, day out', but that didn't seem to matter to the health of their memory as long as they felt they could count on their partner.

In summary, good, close relationships are fantastic for our health and well-being. When we are happy and positive, we feel vitalised and content. Simple things like replacing screen time with people time, livening up relationships by doing something new together – long walks, date nights – all add to our feelings of completeness. Family feuds take a terrible toll on our health and well-being; building bridges may well improve physical and mental health. This wisdom is not new, but we always need reminding here and there that happiness, connection and forgiveness are paramount for our health.

I find the Harvard study fascinating. We focus so much on the physical when it comes to health – am I exercising enough, eating the right food, taking the correct vitamins, how's my cholesterol? Of course , these are important, but the single most essential factor may be the way we interact with other people and the world.

AUTHENTICITY AND TRUTH

Being authentic and telling the truth are two of the fundamentals of happiness. When you just follow the crowd, you are lost.

I love this quote from Mahatma Gandhi:

> 'Happiness is when what you think, what you say and what you do are in harmony.'

There is real truth to this. It's easy to be agreeable to keep the peace; many people are so busy and overloaded that they simply go along with things that don't resonate with them, even things that they know are wrong in some way. Unfortunately, not speaking your truth is one of the fundamentals behind anxiety. Thoughts go around and around in your mind like a merry-go-round, keeping you up at night and compromising your sleep. Not standing in your power causes long-term stress as you can't shake the feeling, which in turn rots your body, allowing physical weaknesses to bloom into dis-ease. We know that stress is a major component of dis-ease, so limiting it where possible is paramount.

Limiting stress isn't about hiding your head in the sand; keeping the peace ultimately simply ignites an internal war. Having integrity and clear boundaries with others but also with yourself is critical for health.

My core belief and value is to: 'Do the right thing because it's the right thing to do'.

This is not an easy way to live; in the outside world, it is far easier to follow the crowd and get on with it, but ultimately, if it doesn't feel right, it's damaging to your health. Not speaking up takes a huge toll on your mental, spiritual and physical well-being.

If you are on the spiritual path, as many people are, you will have to tell the truth no matter how hard it is to do so. Bravery underpins the spiritual path. You can still have tact – there is no need to be rude – but when something needs saying, you must have the inner strength to speak up. When you do, you find your tribe, and can be the light for others. It's incredible how many people are quietly on the spiritual path but don't tell others. Those who are, need to speak up about it, because when you stand in your power and start talking about your loves, and what really matters, you ignite the truth in others too. You awaken their light and find kinship. The more authentic you are, the less of your life force will be tied up in fretting about what you did or did not say, which in turn means you will have more energy. Authenticity is key to happiness and high energy!

> 'A girl should be two things: who and what she wants.'
>
> Coco Chanel

The world is a rocky place at the moment; it's jarring and unsettling. The ground seems to keep moving. Truth anchors you, it gives you strength, it allows you to feel proud of yourself. Shame is such a destructive emotion and one that, unfortunately, eats away at people, sometimes indefinitely.

Deception and lack of truthfulness will destroy your friendships and reputation. It will be far harder for people to connect to you and for you to connect with yourself. The more authentic and truthful you are, the more centred you will feel. Keeping your word means you don't have to stress about not keeping it, which causes anxiety. If you act with integrity by doing the right thing, shame vanishes from your future.

If you are ready to be joyful, say what you mean and mean what you say.

ENERGY HACK

I want you to write a list of 26 things that excite you, preferably not high-ticket items but ones that are either free or low-cost. The world is at your fingertips, you can experience wonderful things that bring joy daily. I want you to commit to doing one of the things that make you happy every week for the rest of the year. This energy hack will bring you happiness to help you feel spiritually fulfilled and energetic.

Remember – stress is the nemesis of happiness. We live in a world that never switches off. Many of us feel that we have to be ready to run from or fight impending danger at any moment. Danger is everywhere – the unyielding deadline, traffic, a row with a friend or lover, the news.

When we are stressed, we cannot repair ourselves physically. The less stressed you are, the more happiness you invite and the healthier you will be, physically, mentally and energetically. Even if you have a stressful life overall, finding five minutes a day to sit quietly will help; and the more quiet time you have, the better.

You as much as anyone deserve a life full of happiness. A life where joy radiates from every cell in your body. A life in which stress no longer has a free pass to drain your energy and your soul, preventing you from doing what brings peace, fulfilment and even bliss. If you nourish your body from the inside, you are going to see positive changes throughout every element of your life. Soon you will see that changes you make to your eating habits, for example, along with a new focus on finding happiness and nourishing your relationships, will have a big effect on your health, vitality and your mindset.

You will need all this energy because you are about to enter the most exciting chapter of your life. I'm going to arm you with the knowledge and the tools you need to fiercely edit your life, your social circles and the energy you're loading into your body. You have the power to change how you feel, it's up to you and it will be wonderful!

1 How have I been spending the two hours before bed? Instead, what practices or exercises can I try that will make me feel calm and quiet?

....

....

....

....

....

2 For a week, throughout the day, I will observe how much of the day I really enjoy. Write down how much of your day gave you joy.

....

....

....

....

....

3 I will pay attention to my interactions with family and friends and observe their quality and how much they do or don't nourish and support me. Are there any patterns?

....

....

....

....

....

4 What are my favourite simple, whole foods that I will enjoy eating for a week?

....

....

....

....

....

5 Where do I like to walk?

....

....

....

....

....

CHAPTER FIVE

Grounding, Meditation and Energy Work in Nature

This chapter is a workbook of exercises that will relax, unwind and de-stress even the most hardened city slicker. Connecting to nature can be done in a plethora of ways, and here I'm going to show you how. Nature is incredibly important to me; it affects my outlook, my energy and my mindset. I'm an ex-Londoner who lived in the hustle and bustle of Bayswater, then Finsbury Park, for over twenty years. A twenty-year stint; it sounds like a prison sentence! Residing in a flat, I had to find ways to bring the outside in and connect to nature, to relax amid chaos. With so many people living on top of each other, city life can drive you nuts. Everyone's energies are muddled together, a lot of emotion and drama. I can't count the number of times I heard arguments and sobbing on the street outside my home, plus fights, as well as laughter.

Whether you live in a flat or a house it's important that you understand that you can be affected by other people's energy; emotion is contagious. Hanging out with an anxious person can make you nervous, and a depressed person can put you in a funk. Conversely, a happy person nourishes you and brightens up your day, and laughter feeds the soul. You feel more alive and joyful around radiators. Cities are melting pots of culture and also of emotion. If you can keep your head while those around you are losing theirs (to coin a phrase), you will maintain your happiness and health, even though not everyone you live near or encounter in your area is going to be as focused on having positive energy as you.

Don't forget that you already have the knowledge on how to cleanse your house with herbs and dispel any bad energies that have lingered. Meditation and grounding are vital to everyone but can be particularly valuable if you live in an urban environment surrounded by people. Finding your peace when the world feels chaotic is a superpower.

MEDITATION: EASIER THAN YOU MAY THINK!

Remember, the brain needs a break; like all energy sources it needs to recharge and rest, and meditation is great for this. Nature provides a beautiful canvas for you to meditate in and on. The Earth is quite literally full of energy that you can soak up wherever you are in the world. Couple this with meditation and you are onto a winner! Did you know meditation comes in many forms and can look many different ways? It's not just about sitting on a mountain in full lotus stilling the mind. You could take a barefoot walk through your local park focusing only on your walking; this is also a form of meditation, one that is really picking up pace with busy city dwellers who don't have access to private outside space like a garden. Here are my top tips to help guide you in starting or improving your meditative practice; you may even discover that you are meditating already without realising it!

- Guided meditations can be wonderfully helpful. They are abundant on YouTube, or you could invest in an app like Calm or Head Space.
- If you lose yourself in music, when you are at one with it, you are meditating! You know that feeling when your jam comes on and you are really in the groove. Meditation is about connecting. You are meditating if you are dancing – if you're just having

fun, rather than posing or forcing it. You can even meditate while doing chores. Doing the dishes or cleaning are ideal times; play your favourite songs and have a boogie.

- Tasks that are fun and flowing are meditative as they require less of your concentration. Skills you are naturally drawn to are meditative; that might be anything from sports to nature to cooking. Any time you stop overthinking and live in the moment is meditative. When you are doing this, you are feeding yourself with positive energy!
- Morning walks as the sun rises are brilliant for your mental health. Start your day off right with gratitude and a walk for a natural boost of energy. Plus, if you go for a daybreak walk you will have a head start on the day, which will leave you feeling positive, accomplished and ready to tackle your tasks head-on.
- Anything that gets you out of your head into your heart or connecting beyond yourself is meditative. 'Follow your bliss' – do what nourishes you, what makes you feel warm and fuzzy inside.

Throughout the rest of this chapter, I will show you all sorts of techniques to energetically connect you with yourself more deeply. As you read through, you can note down the techniques that resonate with you and pick a few to do. They could be as simple as a daily walk in nature or listening to your favourite songs and dancing around the living room as a form of meditation. Daily actions become habits; habits become lifestyle. A good lifestyle will feed and nourish your life force and boost your energy.

GROUNDING

Grounding or earthing is a simple, accessible and free well-being practice. All you need to do to ground is touch the Earth with your feet. When you stand on natural surfaces, such as grass or sand, a current is created between you and the Earth; it's like a battery. Negative ions (which are the good ones) are transmitted into you, and you release positive ions (the less good ones).

Now for the geeky bit. Positive ions are molecules that have lost one or more of their electrons in their outer shell. Conversely, negative ions oxygenate atoms with extra-negatively charged electrons. Negative ions are abundant in nature, especially around waterfalls, on the ocean surf and on the beach, and are also widespread in mountains and forests. Negative ions are a big part of what makes you feel good when you spend time in nature.

How Do You Know If You Are Ungrounded?

If you live in the countryside or near the sea, you may be fortunate enough to be grounded passively. If you are a city dweller but spend significant time outside in places like parks, you may also be grounded. Dog owners tend to be more grounded as they are outside with their pet at least once a day for walks. Walking in parks or wooded areas, naturally soaking up negative ions and releasing positive ones. (This is part of the reason pets are soothing; they also ground us in their own right, and taking care of other beings is also good for the soul: more on that later.)

Below is a checklist. If you suffer from two or more of the following, you may want to make efforts to spend more time in nature.

- Being easily distracted: do you find it hard to concentrate? Does your mind skip from task to task? Can you focus on the project at hand, or do you find yourself thinking about something else entirely? Can you read a book or long article without mentally wandering off? Can you retain the information you read, or do you have to re-read it several times?
- Feeling 'spaced out': we all feel spaced out occasionally, but if it's a regular occurrence for you, grounding might help.
- Overthinking and getting stuck in brain loops: if you find yourself reliving the past and playing out scenes in your head, maybe coming up with the perfect response days, weeks, months or years later, get outside! Ruminating endlessly on past mistakes, abuse

or grievances is not healthy. It's better to talk it out and release it.

- Being a drama queen: do you overreact and throw your toys out of the pram regularly? Do you get easily triggered or have tantrums? Have you noticed that you are much more chilled out when you are away on holiday on a beach or in the countryside or mountains? Of course, on holiday you don't have the pressures of work or everyday life, but another reason for how easily you flip out could be a lack of grounding, especially if you live in a tower block or other urban setting.
- Are you a worry wart or a nervous Nelly? Are you anxious? Perpetually living in the future, playing out worst-case scenarios, 99 per cent of which will never happen? Be aware of your thoughts, as thoughts are intentions, and intentions are wishes or orders to the universe. Remember, energy flows where your intention goes, so you may unwittingly be manifesting or building a reality you wish to avoid. I will cover this in greater detail in the chapter on manifesting.
- Being easily deceived: how discerning are you? Can you tell when people are fibbing, and do you lie to yourself? If your internal lie detector is on the fritz, it could be because you are ungrounded. When you are better connected to yourself and nature, you can better detect when others are attempting to pull the wool over your eyes.

- Obsession with personal image: extreme vanity is a sign of being ungrounded. Social media has made most of us more narcissistic, to the detriment of our mental health. Vanity is not new, though: Narcissus was a Greek god who fell in love with his reflection in a spring. He was so enamoured with himself that he drowned while admiring his own image. Narcissus' tale reminds us not to be too vain, or a dark fate may befall us. The more self-centred we are, the lonelier we ultimately become.
- Do you feel physically that you're not your best? If you have difficulty sleeping, have gained weight or heal slowly from wounds, you may need to ground. I'll tell you exactly how to do so a little later in this chapter.

'If you are depressed, you are living in the past. If you are anxious, you are living in the future. If you are at peace, you are living in the moment.' I love this quote, although its origin is debated. Do you feel a constant need and desire for material things and possessions? Are you overly concerned with labels and image? I get it, we all like nice things, but if they are beyond your means and you are getting into debt, you may have a problem. Any time you find yourself looking for happiness in the bottom of a shopping bag, you may want to get in touch with yourself and nature again.

What Are the Benefits of Being Grounded?

Physical benefits include reduced inflammation. Inflammation is the foundation of many illnesses.

According to the University of Queensland, Australia: 'Inflammation is a response present in many diseases – it is the reason for your sore throat and runny nose when you have a cold, for example.'[1]

Chronic inflammatory diseases include:

- Fatty liver disease
- Endometriosis
- Type 2 diabetes mellitus
- Type 1 diabetes mellitus
- Inflammatory bowel disease (IBD)
- Asthma
- Rheumatoid arthritis
- Obesity
- Alzheimer's
- Parkinson's disease and even cancer.

I'm not claiming grounding can cure any of these diseases; however, it's clear that the less inflamed we are, the better. If walking on the beach or grass promotes wellness, why the heck not do it? You may have even noticed that when you go on holiday to the seaside, country or mountains, for the first few days you pee like a racehorse! This is because you excrete retained water; water retention is linked to inflammation.[2]

Being grounded can also help with weight loss and reduction in pain. Grounding is said to help you lose weight by reducing stress and cortisone levels. In a small human trial, all participants in the group who grounded for 15 minutes a day for ten weeks lost weight, regulated their appetite and reported reduced stress.

The same group:

- improved mood
- improved sleep
- improved energy levels
- reduced chronic-pain issues
- increased activity level overall
- significantly reduced stress levels in their lives
- normalised their appetites and reduced cravings.[3]

Studies have even found that grounding helps you recover from wounds faster.

How can you ground? Grounding can be as simple as connecting to the Earth by walking barefoot on grass, the beach, or any natural surface. If it's wet, all the better, as water is conductive. The optimal way to ground is walking barefoot in the sea; it's a double whammy. Saltwater is a superconductor, so you have the salty benefits of the sea, which I will discuss later in this chapter, plus you are connected to the Earth via the sand. Ensure the surface is natural; walking on paving stones, concrete or AstroTurf won't have the same benefits. If barefoot walking isn't for you, you could always invest in some suede moccasins; if you can handle them being wet, you will reap more benefits. Suede is a natural material that allows electrons to flow through it, unlike rubber soles. As water is conductive, when they are wet you get more benefits via electron exchange. Grounding shoes – shoes with conductive soles – are also available. You could try Earth Runners, or search online.

If you live a busy life and getting out into nature isn't a regular occurrence, you could always invest in some grounding products. I live by the motto 'work smarter, not harder', so grounding products really work for me. The idea is to gain the benefits of grounding without extra effort on your part. Making situations work for you by passively grounding.

Electricity needs grounding to ensure that you don't electrocute yourself. Plug sockets in the UK have a prong that is grounded into the earth for our safety. There are sheets, blankets and mats available that you plug into a wall socket; they only have the top prong, the earthing one, so no electricity flows through them. I have a small grounding mat and a large mat that goes under my bottom sheet. Grounding while you sleep is ideal. No effort, yet all the benefits.

If you are outdoorsy and have the opportunity to get outside, you may be able to connect with nature directly without needing devices. I live in Cornwall these days and am lucky enough to go surfing several days a week. The sessions usually last for two hours and I find being in the sea that long is the ultimate way to ground. Natural water is a brilliant place to ground; swimming or paddling in the sea, a lake or a river is ideal.

FOREST BATHING AND BREATHING

Forest bathing (shinrin-yoku) is a Japanese concept and a fantastic, easy, free way to ground. Simply go to a forest and take a mindful walk for at least two hours. Tell whoever you need to that you will be incommunicado and switch your phone off. If you are going on a particularly long hike or don't know your way, you could follow a trail or use a paper map. You could walk with a friend, but if you want to maximise benefits, keep chatter to a minimum. Or walk alone. Ensure you go out in the morning, or at least early enough in the day that it won't get dark before you finish; remember to take water and snacks.

Ensure your walk is within your fitness limits; check the distance and the difficulty level beforehand. Don't be afraid to rest, or to turn back if it gets too much. Work up to longer walks as your fitness and strength increase. Check the weather forecast; walking in the rain may be less pleasurable (although it has benefits, as you will learn later) and could be treacherous or hazardous. If you don't feel like being too isolated, you could walk around a botanical garden or a wooded park. The idea is to be around as many plants and as few people as possible.

Make the effort to get up early and observe the sunrise. Looking at the sun at sunrise or sunset is a beautiful way to absorb photons – particles of light. Enlightenment is about cultivation of light. You may have noticed when a friend falls in love they are more radiant – they almost glow. That's because there is love shining from their heart and light shining from their body. People who are spiritually awake also radiate love and beam out more light, so the more light you can absorb, the better. Staring at the sun at other times of the day can damage the retina, so stick to sunrise and sunset.

Avoid thinking about your to-do list, be present in the moment, drink in your surroundings. This is your time; everything else can wait.

Calmly walk, hike or stroll your trail. Pay attention to your breath. Being in nature is the best time to release the stagnant air in your lungs and replace it with fresh air.

1. Let go of all the breath in your lungs, breathe out until there is no breath left.
2. Inhale through your nose, first filling the abdomen so your belly pops out, then fill your lungs completely.
3. Strongly exhale through your mouth, emptying your lungs and abdomen.
4. Continue this belly breathing, repeating steps 2 and 3 for 30 breaths.

The more fresh air you have in your lungs, the more alive you will feel, so if you combine forest bathing with breathwork, you will nourish your body, mind and soul especially deeply.

You will probably notice, while forest bathing your surroundings engage every sense. Take the time to smell the roses – literally, smell all the flowers and plants. What can you smell? How many shades of green can you see? People relax the most when looking at shades of green and blue, which is why there are traditionally blue or green rooms backstage on TV sets and in some hospitals.

How does it feel to touch the plants, trees and Earth? Are there any berries that you recognise you can nibble on? (Never eat a berry you are unfamiliar with; if you are unsure, take a book to help you identify or let them be.) I often find blackberry bushes on walks, and pick the abundant fruit; foraging is another excellent way to connect to nature. Pick flowers or herbs on your adventures. Be mindful though not to take too much, don't pick anything belonging to another person and never trespass onto private land.

What can you hear? Are birds singing, leaves rustling, can you hear other wild sounds? Can you identify any plants, trees or flowers? Which ones? Take a mental note of them. Look at the clouds; what shapes, sizes and colours are they? Is there a mighty tree you are particularly drawn to? Some trees are better grounders/ion traders than others. Older and bigger ones tend to work the best, as their root network has often spread far and wide. I was on a hike recently with a friend when my intuition told me to hug a particular tree. It was truly invigorating as the energy rushed into me. That tree made us both a little high, which was unexpected.

If you feel drawn to a tree, sit or stand by it, lean against it or hug it, if you feel brave. Tree hugging may sound a little too hippy to some, but it can help to ground you, especially if done barefoot. Think of the battery idea once again – the tree will pull positive ions out of you and replace them with negative ions, uplifting you.

When grounding through your feet, you only have the relatively small surface area of your feet touching the grounding surface. If you hug a tree, all the parts of your body in direct contact with it are swapping ions all at once, so it's more bang for your buck. Give it a go, hug a tree, I dare you!

COLD-WATER THERAPY

Note: if you go cold-water swimming without the proper training, you risk hypothermia. Proceed with caution and only once fully informed.

Wild cold-water swimming is all the rage these days; the Beckhams recently installed a 'status lake' at their home, and Ed Sheeran has a 'nature pond'. Icy dips are a favourite of Fearne Cotton, Russell Brand, Nicole Scherzinger, Amanda Holden, Holly Willoughby and Joe Wicks, to name but a few. Groups around the UK meet daily to brave the chilly seas. The Cornish Atlantic is a bracing average of 7 degrees Celsius (or 44 degrees Fahrenheit) in winter, which has earned the group who swim in it the title 'The Blue Tits' for women and 'The Blue Balls' for chaps.

I look at them in disbelief as I surf in my 5mm wetsuit, gloves, boots and hood. Even during the summer,

Cornish waters only reach a not-so-balmy 18 degrees on average, making cold-water therapy of various extremes accessible to me at any point.

People also immerse themselves in Baltic ice baths (very cold water), working their way up to 15 minutes, which is the maximum from a safety perspective. If you can manage ten or more, you are doing very well.

If you feel heroic, you could brave the British sea or an ice bath. You may, however, want to start by dipping your toe in, so to speak, and simply turning the temperature down at the end of your shower for 15 seconds and build from there. Do what feels right for you.

Some of the benefits of cold-water exposure:

- Improves metabolism: a cold shower two to three times a week can increase your metabolism and help you lose weight over time. Brown fat, AKA adipose tissue, AKA the body's fuel reserves, is activated and burned when you get cold, producing heat to keep you warm in colder conditions. Cold exposure can increase your metabolic rate 25–40 per cent, so having cold showers regularly can quite literally make you lean.
- Boosts circulation: cold water stimulates blood flow as the blood rushes to the vital organs. Your heart is forced to pump more efficiently, pushing blood through your vessels and supplying every part of your body with much needed oxygen and nutrients. Regular

cold showers promote circulation and a healthy body.

- Enhances the immune system: cold water can boost your immune system as the lymphatic system can stagnate, especially if you don't exercise regularly. When you immerse yourself in cold water, the lymph vessels contract, forcing the fluid around the body and flushing out waste. Cold-water exposure even triggers leukocytes (white blood cells) to attack and destroy unwanted substances in the lymph. This means you are better able to fight off bugs and infections.
- Elevates your happiness: cold-water exposure can help with depression or low mood, as the water triggers mood-enhancing neurotransmitters that make you feel happy.
- Improves mental clarity and reduces brain fog: if you are stuck in a mental spiral, obsessing about your past or future, then cold-water swimming or a cold shower will perk you up and focus your mind.
- Reduces inflammation and swelling: if you want to reduce inflammation, cold water can do that too, as it lowers the damaged tissues' temperature and constricts the blood vessels. Athletes commonly have a cold soak after a hard training session as it's been proven to reduce DOMS (delayed onset muscle soreness).
- Beneficial for beauty: finally, a brisk, cold swim stimulates hair follicles, which can increase hair health and thickness; it can even make hair shinier, as well as tightening your skin and reducing pore size.

Cold-water therapy is invigorating; it boosts your energy and happiness, filling up your reserves so you have more spring in your step and love to give.

> 'Cold-water swimming in nature brings you to the deepest part of yourself, reconnection of body and mind, just like a deep form of meditation.'
>
> Laura Hof – Icewoman

It should be noted that cold-water swimming and ice baths are not a cure-all or suitable for everyone, and if you have recently been released from hospital, are immune-compromised or have a heart condition, they should be avoided; it's essential to know your body and limits. Talk to a medical professional if in any doubt.

Otherwise, with all those benefits, are you ready to take the chilly plunge?

SALTY GOODNESS – HALOTHERAPY

Salt has had a bad reputation in recent times and many health resources tell us to cut back or to avoid it. High levels of salt in your diet may well be bad, but good-quality salt in your lifestyle may have more benefits than you thought.

Breathing in salt minerals can reduce stress levels, improve breathing and enhance your skin's condition.

The benefits of salt were recognised as far back as 1843 when Polish doctor Feliks Boczkowski noticed that men working in salt mines were healthy and thriving, with very few respiratory issues. Brits have been enjoying the benefits of salty air since Victorian times, when the seaside became popular for holidays and to boost wellness. More modern research has found that microscopic particles of natural salt ease respiratory difficulties and boost well-being.[4]

Benefits of salt therapy include:

- Reduction in conditions including eczema, sinusitis, hay fever, asthma and other breathing issues.
- Boosting the immune system and increasing lung function.
- Natural salt contains our friends, negative ions, which help the body relax, elevate mood, aid with weight loss and improve sleep.
- Improved energy levels and sharpened concentration.
- Salt is healing, which you will know if you have ever gargled with salt for a sore throat. When you breathe in salty air, your lungs get antibacterial and antiviral benefits.

Visits to salt caves have become popular in recent years; they are a fully immersive experience, relaxing and excellent for boosting health. If you don't live near one or the seaside, you could invest in a salt lamp. These are natural and pleasant to look at, with their pretty pink glow and are thought to help improve air quality, enhance your mood, and help you sleep. They are an easy way to passively reap some of the benefits of salt.

For a more substantial salty hit, you could opt for a salt pipe or inhaler. I recommend you fill it with Himalayan salt or halite (rock salt) crystals. These salts have a high mineral content, which, it is claimed, give you the benefits of the minerals, including potassium, magnesium and calcium, as well as the salt or sodium. When using the device, slowly breathe in through your mouth and out through your nose.

If you want to connect inwards and maximise the salty benefits of negative ions, a flotation tank might be for you. Flotation tanks are big baths with lids. The water is heated to 35 degrees Celsius (or 95 degrees Fahrenheit), which is the temperature of your skin. They are loaded with Epsom salts, which make you float easily, and are soundproof, calming places. If you need a little grounding and 'me time', especially in the city, they are a godsend.

The following are some of the benefits of flotation tanks:

- Stimulate the release of endorphins.
- Create calm and total relaxation.
- Rejuvenate the mind and body.
- Alleviate mental and physical stress.

- Help with fatigue and jet lag.
- Improve sleep and insomnia.

OTHER TECHNIQUES TO CONNECT YOU WITH NATURE

If you want to improve the energy in your work or home environment, try making offerings to nature spirits, also known as fae. Fruit, flowers, candles and incense all work well. You could make a shrine in the garden in the same kind of way as you might leave out cookies and milk for Santa on Christmas Eve. Put the sweet offerings in a place in your garden that feels right or, if you don't have one, put them by a pot plant or in a window box.

If you want to increase your well-being and improve your karma, and have access to a garden or yard, feed and watch birds. Put out a bird bath and an insect drinking plate. Sow flowers for bees, create a place for hedgehogs to spend their winter or for bats to sleep during summer days. Mow your lawn less often and let insects live there. You could get a pet; any time spent playing and caring for animals will boost your well-being.

Simply being kind to others when you have the time and resources will increase your happiness. There is an ancient Sanskrit word, 'seva', which means selfless service: doing something to help others without the thought of reward or what you will get out of it. Being kind or helping simply because the opportunity presents itself; the more you do, the happier you will be.

Perhaps you live in a city or mainly indoors. If so, put a windchime up. This will allow you to notice the wind more.

You could plant seeds or cress; growing plants from seeds, even on a windowsill, will connect you to nature and bring the outside in. The food we produce ourselves is particularly nourishing. If you have access to a garden or allotment where you can grow crops and food , do it.

If you are feeling experimental, you could try something different when growing plants from seeds. Place the seed in your mouth for around a minute, then dig a hole in the soil with your finger. Spit the seed into the hole, top up with saliva and soil and leave it a few days before watering. That seed absorbs your DNA. Supposedly, the plant adapts to you and as it grows, it develops so it contains more of the nutrients that you need; think of it as natural bespoke supplements. Try it with friends or family. When my loved ones and I both experimented with growing tomatoes, mine tasted completely different to theirs!

You could sign up to a farmers' weather forecast email list to keep yourself more aware of the changes of seasons and connect you more deeply to your food.

If you don't have access to nature, bring it in to you. Fill your home with photos or paintings of seascapes, landscapes; collect shells, keep indoor plants and crystals; play soundtracks of nature's sounds. Simply admiring the beauty of nature connects you to it.

If you are fortunate enough to live in a rural location, enjoy the nature that is at your fingertips; if you are a city dweller get into parks. Learn something new about yourself and the world every day by opening up your energy fields, your heart and your mind to its power. Don't put off exploring the natural world that's on your doorstep. Carpe diem (seize the day). Get into nature and start soaking up the goodness all around you, goodness that will fuel every part of your being.

/ What are the energies like in my street/ neighbourhood?

....

....

2 What do I do already that makes me feel like I'm just flowing? What would I like to take up that makes me feel that way?

....

....

....

3 For a week I will notice whenever I feel ungrounded and reflect on why.

....

....

....

4 Is there a cold-water activity nearby that appeals to me?

....

....

5 What selfless service (seva) could I perform?

....

....

6 Three walks near home that I enjoy already or would like to explore:

....

....

....

7 What are three plants/herbs/flowers I would like to grow?

....

....

....

CHAPTER SIX

Manifesting: How to Do It – And the Dark Side

Manifesting is magnificent!

Manifesting will change your life. I know you are going to love the wondrous positivity it will bring. Manifesting truly is a superpower – a superpower that you can easily acquire simply by reading the next few pages. In this chapter we will also look at the dark side of manifesting, which, to the detriment of many, is rarely discussed. I will teach you everything I know about manifesting and the secrets to how it can make your life blessed and happy.

I grew up on the Disney animated movie *Aladdin.* I still exuberantly sing 'A Whole New World' when I'm overexcited. I love the idea of genies, magic lamps and dreams coming true. What if Aladdin was based on more than pure fantasy? What if all your wishes could come true?

The word 'abracadabra', synonymous with the stories of Aladdin, has a hotly debated meaning. Some say it's gibberish; I prefer the explanation that it comes from the Aramaic – 'abra' or 'avra' meaning 'I will create', and 'cadabra' or 'kedoobra' meaning 'as was spoken'. 'I will create as was spoken' or 'I create what I say' – which is 'manifesting'! Thoughts create every single thing; all objects were born from an idea. Thoughts are energy and energy is something *you* can master!

Everything man-made goes through three stages of manifestation. All products go from a gas to a liquid to a solid. I will explain it all so you can better understand the importance of your thoughts and the incredible power they have to shape your present and your future life. Thoughts are the foundation of every single element of your life. The good and the bad. Thoughts become things, which is why mastery of the mind and your thoughts is so important in the enlightening process. Everything starts with the energy of your thoughts – what you think radiates back to you in more ways than you know. Later in the book I will teach you how thoughts also manifest dis-ease, in the Grand Theory of Dis-ease chapter, where we look in detail at my theory of solid–liquid–gas, which is fundamental to spiritual evolution. For now, though, I want to share a snapshot that will teach you the secrets of how manifesting truly works. The hidden knowledge of how *you* can easily and quickly become a master manifester!

Stage 1. Everything starts with a thought, an idea. Think of the world of product design. A pen, a phone, a car, a plate, a pool – all of these are initially dreamed of in someone's mind. Somebody visualises how the thing will look.

Thoughts and emotions, in my theory, are gases. Emotion simply means energy in motion. People radiate emotions; you can immediately feel if someone is happy or sad from the energy they emit. The same goes for thoughts and ideas. An idea before it's a 'thing' is simply a concept, a vision; formless, in the ether – a gas.

Stage 2. The liquid stage. The planning, drawing and design stage. Before items go into production, they are all designed. Sometimes this is done with a pen and paper; the paper is solid but the ink is liquid, the design flows. In other cases, design starts on a computer. Computers have a solid shell, but a liquid screen.

Stage 3. The building stage. This is where all the components are combined to create the designer's item in physical form – solid form. Whether it's a pen, a phone, a car, someone thought of it (gas), someone designed it (liquid) and they made it (solid).

So, the car you drive, the pair of jeans you are wearing now, the chair you are sitting on, the building you go to work in and everything else that is man-made – all started as 'just' an idea. A thought in someone's mind that was then designed and planned. Someone worked out how exactly it would look, feel and operate. This was probably executed on a liquid screen. Then it was made real, built in the physical world.

Every single man-made item goes through these stages. It is the creation and manifesting process. It all starts with single thought – the spark of inspiration.

Be present and precise with your thoughts and what you write – words have power. Think of the word 'spelling'; what does it really mean? Spelling literally means to create spells. Writing and designing is stage two of manifesting; if you want something to happen, start by writing it down (we will look more at this later).

You may remember that the 90s were characterised by *The Secret*. The movie and book both inspired a generation. It was the first time that the 'Law of Attraction' wisdom was in the mainstream. The principle is simple: like magnetically attracts like. Whatever thoughts or vibes you radiate come back to you. If you want love, you need to project love; if it's wealth or abundance you desire, you need to project that.

The problem is that it's very hard to get into a loving mindset if you are feeling unlovable. If you are worried about bills, it's hard to come from an abundance stance. If you're not totally clear about what you're asking for, you won't get it. It's as simple as that.

HOW TO CONFUSE THE UNIVERSE AND ORDER WHAT YOU DON'T WANT!

The following story is an example of how important positive thoughts and clear vision are to manifesting.

Imagine you're going to a restaurant. You want steak; it has been on your mind all week and you are excited about your delicious, nutritious dinner. You sit down, chat with your friends, order a drink and peruse the menu. Sirloin, rib-eye, fillet? What sides? What sauce? You think it all through until you can visualise your whole dinner – visualise it being put down in front of you for you to enjoy. You can't wait! Then, happy with your decision, you make your order. Once the waiter has gone, you no longer need to think about it, safe in the knowledge that the kitchen team are beavering away.

If you do this – decide on your order, or energetically 'set the intention' in manifesting terms, and order it with focus – the universe (the waiter and kitchen) will bring your order (your wish) to fruition. However, people often add an extra step: a negative, self-sabotaging step. Imagine you arrive at the restaurant wanting steak, but then see a chicken dish on the menu that sounds good too. When the waiter comes to take your order, you don't have a clear picture of your dinner arriving on the table. You mutter about the chicken, then about the steak. You keep flipping between the two, never really giving the waiter a clear order. The waiter doesn't know what to write down. The busy kitchen don't know how many steaks and how many chicken dishes they should be prepping. When the waiter walks by, you ask to change your order again and again. It's all very confusing. Eventually the waiter, in despair, offers to choose for you, which seems like the best option. When the chicken arrives your heart sinks. It wasn't really what you wanted, so you feel disappointed.

Be precise about what you want, and visualise it, then order it. Don't self-sabotage by being unclear. Know what you want and stick to it. Stop focusing on things you don't want; instead, focus on things you do want!

This concept applies to whatever you're manifesting: whatever you are thinking about, or wishing for. Whatever you are consistently focused on will find you. You need to be clear about what it is you want to invite in. If you desire more material wealth but you focus on your lack of it, you will attract a continuing lack of it. If you are not clear on what you are ordering, like in that restaurant, you will probably end up with something you don't want. The Aladdin story shows us what happens when the genie misinterprets wishes and brings too much of something, or the wrong thing. The precision of language and of desire, or intention, is key. Be careful what you wish for, because you just might get it, is the message.

THE DARK SIDE OF MANIFESTING

We are all constantly manifesting. As we've already covered in this chapter, the law of attraction causes you to attract what's in your energetic field. In other words, what you are thinking about. The more you think about it, the more thought energy (gas) you put into it and the faster it arrives. What's missing from this model is the awareness of what is in your subconscious and energetic field. If you have not entirely come to terms with events from your childhood, for example, you may unwittingly be ordering more of them from the universe, meaning that history will, unfortunately, repeat itself. This is often mistaken for 'karma', but to me it's simply not processing your trauma and therefore continuing to order suffering from the universe. This is what I refer to as the dark side of manifesting. The only way to get out of vicious cycles like this is to completely forgive and be at peace with the repeating pattern, starting with the first time it happened. It could be that you haven't thought about the issue or event for years, but if the same situation keeps playing out repeatedly with different people in different contexts, you need to get to the bottom of it to move forwards and live a happy life. If you have grown up in a home with infidelity, for example, cheating will be in your energetic field, even if it wasn't you doing the cheating. Simply living in a home where it was happening is enough for the energetic signature of infidelity to imprint on you. This may sound harsh but it's vital for you to understand why this keeps happening so you can correct course and start to order things you do want rather than more tough times. Knowledge is power, and it's time for you to start to use the law of attraction in your favour to welcome in the life you want, the life you deserve.

You already know that you have been attracting some of the wrong things – now you know why and how you are doing it. The good news is that now you can take charge, and own your future happiness. You need to be mindful of all your thoughts from this moment onwards, so that you don't invite any more negative elements into your life. Forgiveness is key. You need to let go of a past that haunts you, especially if you see history repeating itself. Keep your thoughts positive, and daydream your wishes into existence. More on this later.

THE LIGHT SIDE OF MANIFESTING

We can turn our attention now to the lighter side of manifesting – this is where the fun begins! When it comes to the lighter side of manifesting, just as with the dark, always remember: like attracts like – kindness attracts kindness; happiness will attract more happiness. When you are happy, you are complete; you are open to more amazing things happening to you and your life. Your energy is radiant, your being is lit up from the inside out – you are glowing. It's time to show you how to amplify your glow-up!

It's Genie Time – How to Manifest

The techniques below need to be done away from distractions, when you can entirely focus and engage with them, not when you are thinking about a thousand other things and have kids zooming about. Carve out some 'me' time. If you have a to-do list stressing you out, do some of that. If you are distracted or under pressure, your results will be limited. These two steps can be used for any blocked area in your life where you wish to manifest a better tomorrow, but for this exercise, I will focus on lack of abundance.

Step 1: Letting Trauma Go

Step one is for the brave, those who are ready and willing to be accountable for their actions, even though this may prove uncomfortable. Warriors with the resolve to face up to their past and become victors, not victims. Those who have suffered hardship, sometimes truly heartbreaking events. Those willing to let go of their suffering so their history won't muddy their future. Remember: if you don't let go of your past, you are doomed to create more of the same. If you want to know what your future looks like, look at the choices you are making right now. Either you go after the life you want or keep settling for the life you get.

Of course, the hardships you endured may not have been your fault; others may have hurt, upset or abused you. However, your current and future happiness are solely your responsibility. If you are not ready to deal with your history, please advance to step two and return to this step when you feel emotionally strong enough to forgive. Alternatively, please seek professional help to let go of the trauma that holds you captive.

For those of you who stayed, I commend your bravery and your openness to becoming the best you.

Let's begin.

Think of a time when money was an issue. Start small. Did you have to budget hard to pay the phone bill? Do you remember a disagreement your parents had about money?

Pick one of these or a similar situation and grade it out of 10, where 10 is the most severe, 2–4/10 is optimal and don't go above a 5. Play the memory in your mind as vividly as possible; when you think of it, you will feel a plethora of emotions: sadness, grief, anger, resentment, sorrow, regret, etc. Now think of either something or someone you deeply love – it might be a partner, child or pet – or maybe the perfect location and day: a sunset, lapping waves, mountains, fields, whatever you most adore.

Next, merge the two scenes. Overlap them and then drown the negative memory in positive thoughts. Sit in that space, melting the negative emotions with the grace of the positive ones. When you are ready, think of your story again. Is the dissonance the same? Is it still rated the same? Or has it gone down by half a point, or even one or more? Notice your progression, note it down and keep repeating these steps until you feel at peace with your past.

NB Please be careful to start small with this technique and get used to it before you tackle more significant issues. Even warriors need training; no one is born a black belt. Once you can neutralise trauma with ease, you can move on to more troubling issues.

Step 2: Daydream Your Way to Abundance

A vivid imagination is the way to manifest your heart's desires. Elite athletes visualise themselves winning again and again, until the frequencies match and the universe has no option but to deliver that reality.

Remember, abracadabra! 'I create what I say'. You need to make the image of your heart's desire as visceral as possible. Engage all your senses.

NB: One thing I've struggled with regarding manifesting is the grammar. As someone born with dyslexia, I can't bear poor grammar because I have had to work so hard to learn it. In traditional manifesting, we are taught to talk as if the thing we want has already happened or already exists: 'I have' rather than 'I want'. I completely understand the reasoning behind this approach – if you use the future tense, you keep your desires as dreams in the perpetual future, like a carrot on a stick, eternally out of reach; but the present-tense grammar creates a disconnect within me.

My workaround is to think and speak about it in terms

of reminiscing about a future memory. I repeat the phrase 'reminisce about a future memory' a lot throughout this section because it's very important; engaging with your dream as though it has already happened is vital. You see and feel it as you would a memory from the past. If you make it yours, as if it already belongs in your memories, you can bring it to fruition.

We have all had brilliant days, maybe on holiday with friends or family, perhaps on your wedding day, or if you ran a marathon or did a skydive? Is the memory a concert or sporting event? The day your child was born? Think about an epic day, in as much detail as possible. Do you remember the weather that day, the sun on your skin, the smell and touch of rain? The colours of the flowers, landscape, buildings or sky? How did you feel? Happy, elated? What did others say? What did you do? What were you wearing, eating, touching?

Now reminisce about a future memory. What do you desire? This can be anything. A relationship, a job, a new home, becoming a champion, winning in court, the holiday of a lifetime . . . I recently used this technique to manifest my dream house – the one I am writing from right now! Here's how to do it.

Reminisce about a future memory. Get into a high vibration. There are various ways to achieve this. You could use the 'attitude of gratitude' by listing the things you are grateful for, in detail, and really feeling thankful. Alternatively, you could think about a person or pet you really love. Get all gooey thinking about them. The more 'loved up' you feel, the more power you will have to manifest. Or simply remember the best day ever and feel the associated happy emotions. Once your vibe is high and you are smiling from within, start to think about your heart's desire. Do not concern yourself with 'how' you will get it; the logistics are for the universe to plan.

Of course, it's not quite Aladdin's lamp and you will need to take active steps to achieve your goals. Prince Charming won't simply materialise in your living room. To meet a partner, be chatty, talk to strangers on the street, strike up conversations with the postman or the cashier, and get used to small talk, so when you meet someone eligible, you don't go bright red and freeze. To Be open to new people, get out into the world, take up a sport or hobby, join a dating site.

If it's a new home you desire, you need to speak to estate agents, put your current home on the market or give your landlord notice and sign up to the relevant websites.

Step 3: Visualise It!

Once you feel happy and gooey, vividly visualise your goal in as much detail as possible.

Reminisce about a future memory. See the house or apartment you want; what can you see? What colour is it? What is it made of? Is it painted, or is it brick? Does it have a driveway? Is it in the countryside or the city, in the mountains or by the sea?

What can you smell as you approach it? The dirt and grit of the city, the freshness of mountain or country air, salt from the sea?

What can you hear? The sound of traffic in a busy city? Waves lapping, sheep bleating, cows mooing? Children laughing? Is music playing?

Can you feel the sun on your skin or the wind in your hair? Notice the shadows and the light.

How does it feel physically? As you approach the door, feel it, see it, touch it, live it.

This is your new home. How do you feel emotionally? Are you excited, happy, elated, ecstatic, even a little apprehensive or overwhelmed?

Feel what you feel, engage every sense. Is there anything to taste or more to smell? Perhaps you can smell fresh coffee or bread baking. Maybe you are drinking or eating those as you explore.

Once through the front door, take a look around and breathe it all in. You will be so happy in your new home, touching the walls and absorbing the colours. What else can you hear, see, smell, taste or touch?

Reminisce about a future memory, make it as vivid, graphic and visceral as possible and wistfully daydream about your heart's desires as if they are already yours. If you are genuinely in that vibration, the universe will deliver it.

> 'Everything is energy and that's all there is to it. Match the frequency of the reality you want and you cannot help but get that reality. It can be no other way. This is not philosophy. This is physics'.
>
> Albert Einstein

MONEY MAGIC: A WORD ON ABUNDANCE

I know some of this abundance may depend a little on financial means; moving house is expensive. I also know that, unfortunately, a large percentage of the spiritual community have been duped into believing that money is somehow evil. In fact, money or abundance creates freedom. When your basic needs are met, you have time to pursue your interests rather than living pay cheque to pay cheque. If you know you can afford your home, food, family, etc. and have some fun along the way, you can learn, grow, explore and choose the kind of life you want.

With money you can get projects off the ground, be innovative and create a beautiful world for yourself and your family. When you are abundant you have more opportunity to be in service to others. When you are stressed about money you may become more insular and self-absorbed. Interestingly, it seems it's true: money doesn't buy you happiness, at least past a certain point. A study found that when you are constantly worried about money, the more you have for a rainy day and to ensure your needs are met, the happier you are. However, once your needs are covered, you don't get any happier. The magic family income reported in the study is $75,000, which is around £62,000 at the time of writing.[1] Those who are in service to self tend to be very money-focused, which is partly why people associate money with evil.

Years ago, as I disembarked from my friend's superyacht in Ibiza and marvelled at his wealth and generosity, he told me a secret: 'If you want money, you need to give it away.' I learned an important lesson that day that has been prominent in my life and my mind ever since: if you give freely without ego or expectation, abundance will find you. Remember, though – don't give recklessly. Only spend what you can afford. Try it out. I would love to know the outcome – reach out to me on social media and let me know. I love hearing wonderful success stories from my followers about how they are improving their lives and how they are thriving, full of energy!

VISION BOARDS

Writing a chapter on manifesting would be impossible without including vision boards. One of my close friends credits vision boards for her extremely opulent lifestyle. She was a relatively 'normal' person who became exceptionally wealthy. She believes in them so much she even threw a Christmas party where her close pals came together and made their own. The components of the house I currently live in are in the vision board I created that day!

The reason vision boards work, goes back to my gas–liquid–solid discovery. If you want something to exist in the physical, you need to guide it there. When you make a vision board, you formulate your thoughts (gas), you next write/draw your intentions with ink (liquid) and finally stick your images to the board, which is solid. You then have it around the house, and each time you walk past it you add more thought energy to it, which draws your desires ever closer.

If you are pressed for time, you could do a quick vision-board hack. Hollywood A-lister Jim Carrey credits his success to manifesting. In an interview he did with Oprah Winfrey, Jim explains how in the mid-80s, when he was broke and not very successful, he used to sit in his car and visualise directors and producers, people he respected in the movie industry, telling him they loved his work. He also wrote himself a cheque for $10 million for 'Acting Services Rendered' and dated it Thanksgiving three years later. He kept it in his wallet, where it got tattier and tattier. Then, just before Thanksgiving 1995, the year written on the cheque, Jim learned he would make $10 million for appearing in *Dumb and Dumber*. This story inspires me, and I have a similar cheque sitting in my wallet as I type. Give it a go. It's all about setting the intention for physical wealth, with a route to it; writing it down and keeping the paper close to you adds more thought energy to it, and so your desires draw ever closer.

NB: You should never expect to obtain wealth without a little effort on your part. *You* need to be part of the solution; it's unlikely to magically appear at your door or in your bank account. What will appear are opportunities – it's up to you to take them.

Vision boards are fun to make, but require a focused flow state. I recommend you set aside some 'me time' to make yours without the distractions of your household. Having a vision-board party, like the one I went to, is also exciting and fun. You could set the scene by playing meditative music, lighting candles and dimming the lights a little. Do what makes you relaxed and focused.

Materials:

- A board or piece of thick card
- Scissors
- Glue
- Art supplies: these could include stickers, feathers,

ribbons, stencils, coloured felt tip pens, tubes of glitter and other sparkly things. I love sparkles, and I think you want to invite as much sparkling and positive energy into your life as possible!

- Images: if you have a stack of old magazines, use those. Or ask friends for theirs, or try your local dentist, hairdresser, nail salon, spa or doctor's surgery, etc. Or, of course, you can buy some; you may find them in second-hand and charity shops. Consider subscribing to mags – it's far cheaper than buying them at the supermarket or newsagent. If you have a magazine subscription, you will have a regular supply and can plan for future boards. Have a root around for postcards, photos, posters and catalogues. Print pictures at home; Pinterest has some wonderful inspirational images. You could even draw your heart's desire or, if you are struggling, simply write it down, although the more inspiring images you have, the better.

When you're thinking about what to include in your board, take a moment to really ask yourself what you are looking for. I like to set questions in my mind and allow the answers to unravel organically over time. I may allocate a day when I will make a vision board in, say, a month's time and start a list of what to include, adding to it as inspiration strikes. I collate images in that way too; if I see a picture that resonates, I take a screenshot of it and add it to a specific folder on my phone or computer. If you want to make your board sooner, simply spend some time sitting quietly and reflecting on what it is you would like to manifest. Vision boards can be seasonal, annual, five-year plans – whatever you need. You can make as many as you want. You could also make one with elements from different timelines – things that are just around the corner and others that might take some time to build. If you have a long-term plan in mind, write the date by which you wish to have achieved your goals at the top of the page.

Do a brain dump of all the things that you desire, no matter how out of reach they feel now, then prioritise them. Which do you want above all else? What do your family life, career and home look like? Have you achieved success in a particular area of your life? What did you do? Let your imagination run wild; it's time to build your dream life and invite an abundance of positive energy in!

It can be easy to focus your vision board solely on material things: monetary gains, a car, a house, etc. For a bit of balance, I recommend you also include elements from the following categories:

- Love: friends and family life.
- Home: where do you live? What does it look like?
- Career: what does your job look like and what goals do you have?

- Bling: the car, the jewellery, the watches, fashion, etc.
- Lifestyle: holidays, sports, hobbies.
- You: how do you want to look and feel? Who do you want to be? What do you want to learn?

Go through your images, searching for the ones that best fit your goals. Cut out more than you need; you are looking for the ones that feel the most inspiring. You may not know which ones they are until you come to make the board. If you have additional images at the end, keep them safe for your next board.

If you can't find the image you are looking for, it's time to go online, search for it, print it or draw it. Select images for each category and choose how you section your board; some boards work from the centre like a pie chart, and others are grids. You may need to crop your images further or cut them out. Remember, you can also draw and write on your board. When you are happy with the basic structure, glue it together, and write inspirational quotes and goals. Finally, add the sparkle – optional.

Some people like to put their boards away and set a reminder on their phone of the date written on them, then pull them out when the reminder goes off to see what they have achieved. Others have their vision board on show and glance at it occasionally. I favour the second approach because you add an extra layer of magic every time you look at it. If you are an anxious person, who would get frustrated that your goals haven't yet appeared, put it away, as you will sabotage or slow down your manifesting – back to being indecisive about the chicken and the steak again.

Your vision board is yours and no one else's. If your priorities change or you achieve your goals, add or take elements away. Your board should be fluid and adaptable.

ENERGY HACK

Change all your logins, website passwords and digital greetings to affirmations. When you log into your bank, have 'I am Blessed' pop up, or log in to Instagram with 'I am well'. Or you could use 'I am happy111', 'I am wealthy222' or 'I am free' as your computer password. Using affirmations, instead of your nickname from college and the year your cat was born, allows you to work smarter, not harder, in a simple and valuable way. They may even be easier to remember!

BILLIONAIRE MINDSET

Billionaires and top CEOs (and elite athletes like those we've mentioned) all have one thing in common. They expect success! They also plan for all eventualities and adjust course accordingly and calmly. Imagine you have taken the time to work through and resolve all the worst-case scenarios. You will never get caught with your proverbial pants down. The universe throws you a curve-ball; you catch it, adjust and move on. Planning is key to success, as is staying calm and collected under pressure. Be a swan. Your legs might be wildly flapping beneath the water, but all we see are grace, calm and beauty.

Successful people expect things to work out, and they usually do. Think again about the law of attraction: if you can't quite decide about the steak and keep changing to the chicken, the chicken is what you will end up with. If you keep stressing about failure, that is what you will manifest.

If you hold the knowing, frequency or resonance of things working out, nine times out of ten, they do. If they don't work out that day, it wasn't your wave; dust yourself off and catch the next one. The more you lament on things that didn't happen, the more time you waste self-sabotaging and rejecting your own happiness.

Anxiety and doubt are like rubbing the genie's lamp and wishing for the worst to happen. Use the strength of your thoughts to power up your dreams rather than destroy them. It's amazing how 'lucky' you become when you believe in yourself.

People on their deathbeds tend to regret not having had the courage to try; you can fail at anything, so you may as well reach for the stars.

ASK, AND YE SHALL RECEIVE

This is one of those things that are obvious but sometimes you need to be told! In my case, it was taught to me by my friend who lives a self-made, beautiful and extremely privileged life. If you want something, ask for it. Worst-case scenario, the answer is no; and if that's the case, so what? Change tack, ask for something else or ask another person. Someone will say yes. You will be surprised how often people do. People generally want to help. You want to help others. It feels good, providing you have the resources to do so.

If you follow these simple steps, the universe will deliver a life of which you have only dreamed. So what's stopping you? Do it now. The sooner you start, the sooner it will be yours. Imagine a life where you are living your dreams, you no longer feel sluggish, you are full of positive energy and it's radiating from your every cell. Let the magic begin!

1 When this week or month did I leave a decision up to someone else and then feel disappointed by it?

....

....

....

....

2 What trauma can I let go of?

....

....

....

3 What is one of my favourite memories?

....

....

....

4 What is one of my favourite future memories?

....

....

....

5 What do I want my first vison board to be about?

....

....

....

6 What can I ask for help with this week?

....

....

....

7 Three ways money makes me able to serve others:

....

....

....

CHAPTER SEVEN

Attitude of Gratitude – How Being Happy Will Make You Well

This chapter is all about gratitude. I will teach you how to start loving yourself and how to cultivate a grateful mindset. The more thankful you are, the stronger your energy and life force will be. You will become more of a radiator and less of a drainer. You will start to ooze good vibes, which will allow your desires to find you. Less chasing, more attracting!

Gratitude is fundamental to abundance, happiness and optimal mental health. When you are grateful, more things tend to go your way and, even when they don't, you are less perturbed. Gratitude has a high vibration, so if you live in a state of gratitude the distance between you and sadness, anger or even stress is vast; it's much harder for you to get upset. You don't tend to sweat the small stuff as much. Life becomes softer and easier; you can glide through it rather than struggle. Cultivating gratitude is fast, simple – and better yet – it's free and you can start today!

HOW AND WHY DOES GRATITUDE WORK?

Regarding gratitude, the universe works in much the same way that humans do.

Imagine spending ages choosing a gift for someone you love. Really considering what they like and who they are. Parting with your hard-earned cash after finding something truly special for them. Looking forward to giving them the present and excited to see their reaction.

There are various ways the receiver can respond to the present; their reaction has consequences.

Reaction One

You hand your buddy the carefully curated present and their response is underwhelming, nonchalant or, worse yet, dismissive and rude. They are ungrateful, or couldn't care less; on to the next present or conversation with barely a whisper of recognition or appreciation.

Reaction Two

As soon as your pal sees that there is a gift, they are excited and grateful, wondering what it is and beaming with appreciation. They open the gift with glee and well up with tears of love and joy. The gift is perfect! They are elated that you truly see them and found them such a wonderful present. They can barely contain their enthusiasm and happiness and hug you, deepening your love and connection.

Consequence

Which scenario do you prefer? Which reaction would make you want to buy more presents for your friend? Which would make you think you might buy gifts for them when it wasn't even their birthday? Silly, cute gifts that you know they will like, gifts that will delight them. Which reaction would make you think you didn't want to buy more gifts for them, wondering what the point would be? Which reaction might even make you think to yourself, what's the point of this friendship when they are that ungrateful?

When it comes to gratitude, the universe works in much the same way as you would in this situation. When you are grateful, the universe wants to give you more things you love; when you get excited and exude thanks and appreciation, the universe feels that and responds by bringing you more things that make you happy.

The universe loves gratitude. When people react positively to things, it responds by providing more and more things to be grateful for. A showering of gifts or an ever-increasing virtuous cycle.

When you react negatively, or don't react at all, the universe doesn't bother sending you things you may like. You are too unpredictable and ungrateful, so what's the point?

This is how gratitude works, so get excited when things go your way and cultivate an attitude of gratitude!

WHAT EXACTLY IS GRATITUDE?

Gratitude isn't about getting what you want; it's about wanting what you have. You don't have to believe in gratitude for it to work. I understand some of you reading this book may be sceptical. I encourage scepticism – it means you are no fool! All I ask is that you accompany your scepticism with an open mind. Try some of the exercises later in this chapter for a week, or better yet a month, and see how you feel. I've seen it work.

Gratitude offers us a way to embrace the fullness of life. Happiness follows gratitude. Happiness is the result of things going your way and everything flowing harmoniously; gratitude is how you get there. With practice, gratitude can be found on even the darkest of days. It is a flickering glow of salvation. Gratitude is a willingness to see the singular beacon of light and feel the goodness beyond it. There will always be a thread of goodness, no matter how bleak things feel. Gratitude is pulling on that thread and ushering in the happiness behind it. The more you seek and cultivate gratitude, the happier and more content you will feel.

Kiss Your Brain: The Science of Gratitude

This is the title of a fascinating Ted Talk by psychologist, instructor and researcher Christina Costa.[1] While working at a school, Christina taught her young pupils to 'kiss their brains', a simple technique whereby they would kiss two fingers and then place them on the top of their heads. A quiet salute to their minds.

Christina then went on to teach older students at college and dropped the practice; she also didn't kiss her own brain for years. When she was diagnosed with anaplastic astrocytoma, a rare and severe brain tumour, everywhere she turned for support, the language was of battles. That she should 'beat the cancer'. That she should picture chemo as an army coming to fight against the cancer cells. The fight narrative was entrenched. Christina knew her tumour might never fully go away and didn't want to think of it in battle terms, as it could be her neighbour for the rest of her life. She didn't want to be at war with her own body.

Christina decided to flip the script: rather than

focusing on what her body had done wrong, she decided to focus on gratitude instead. She read about and investigated gratitude practices and realised that they were similar to what she had been doing when she and her school pupils were kissing their brains.

Christina took every opportunity to focus on the good rather than the bad. Instead of worrying about whether she could have children, she marvelled at how her body produced the perfect quantity of hormones to save eggs for a later date. Every time she had radiotherapy, she kissed her brain and focused on the doctor telling her the healthy cells would repair over time and how the cancer cells could not.

The more Christina practised gratitude, the more peace she found in her situation. She also found, as she explains in her Ted Talk, that science shows that gratitude affects us on a neurological level. When we practise gratitude, happiness increases and depression subsides. Gratitude strengthens our relationships and elevates positive emotions. Interestingly, gratitude also affects us on a physiological level: it strengthens the immune system and even dulls physical pain. When we express gratitude, our brains release dopamine and serotonin, two important neurotransmitters responsible for our emotions and mood, which work by regulating stress hormones. Amazingly, gratitude helps us re-frame potentially destructive thoughts as more positive ones, which makes whatever we are going through a little easier.

As with most things in life, the more we practise gratitude, the easier it becomes. The reason practice makes perfect is due to neuroplasticity, the process by which the brain lays down new circuits to form new pathways. This happens throughout life; anyone, at any point, can adopt a gratitude mindset, and can deepen it over time.

ENERGY HACK

Every day for a month, kiss your first and second finger and then touch your head while thinking loving thoughts towards yourself. Encourage friends and family to do it too and see how you all feel.

Gratitude is unifying. One of the biggest problems we face in society is isolation. It's all too easy for us to feel alone, unseen and unloved.

Remember to kiss your brain and be grateful for all it does for you!

Gratitude is bigger than one individual person; it's the glue that holds society together. Being thankful makes people feel appreciated – a tense situation can become warm and fuzzy in a moment simply by someone expressing gratitude.

Gratitude helps you remember the leg-ups you have had along the way. People have lifted you throughout your life. Taking the time to acknowledge that makes you feel more connected. You realise you are not an island, isolated and alone. You are and have always been part of a community, a collective. You have been helped by thousands of people and have helped thousands of people in both minor and major ways. A random act of kindness can snowball into an avalanche. Choose to always be grateful and kind.

MINDSET

Dr Maurice Duffy is a mindset coach who has worked internationally with sports stars, business leaders and politicians. He spoke to me about the importance of mindset and gratitude. Here are his thoughts.

The single most important factor influencing someone's success, be it personal or professional, is their mindset. What exactly do we mean by this and why is it so important? Your mindset is a set of beliefs that shape how you make sense of the world and yourself. It influences how you think, feel and behave in any given situation. This is important, since what you think about consistently has a direct impact on your behaviour, your choices and your life, not the other way round. So, it is vital to get this fundamental ingredient right. In a nutshell, if you want to be successful, happy and at peace, learn about your own personal mindset. It can make or break your life satisfaction.

Always remember: if you do not consciously adopt a mindset, one will be subconsciously adopted for you. When you become conscious of your mindset, and understand its ways, you can intentionally begin to guide it to help you improve your whole life; it will impact on your physical and mental health, decrease stress and help you become more resilient and happier.

Our minds take in and process the world around us. Depending on the mindset that you adopt on a day-to-day basis, there can be a world of difference in how you approach life – and how life reacts to you. Increasingly, research shows that many of the conditions we once thought of as purely physical problems are, in fact, caused by the way you think and the energy you radiate.

The Whitehall II study asked 7,000 civil servants when they think old age begins.[2] The data showed that those who answered 60 years or less were more likely to go on to develop serious heart problems than those who gave the answer 70 years or more. Often, the only thing standing in the way of success is the perception of your own self and the mindset you choose. If you want to succeed, you must allow yourself to find success by consciously adopting a mindset that works for you. Once you do that, many of the things you want will become available to you.

Many studies have found that those who practise gratitude regularly are 'considerably more satisfied with their lives'.[3] They are happier. Happiness is a choice, not a result. The more grateful you are, the more joy you feel. There's no happier person than a truly thankful, content person. Happiness is a state of mind. All states of mind are generated by your thoughts. Happiness can feel elusive sometimes, especially during the doom and gloom that seems to be growing exponentially at the moment; but gratitude is a surprisingly accessible pathway to contentment, joy and positivity. Take, for example, the study that assessed the autobiographies written early in adult life by 180 Catholic nuns,[4] and which showed a correlation between writing about positive emotions and living a longer life. In fact, the nuns who exhibited positive thinking in their writing lived an average of ten years longer. The power of the mind to control physical health still isn't completely understood, but it seems that there may well be an amazing wealth of power, health and longevity that we can potentially tap into simply by changing our mindset to a more upbeat one.

Here are some top tips to cultivate gratitude and increase your happiness.

- **Start the day right.** Make a conscious decision each morning to be positive.
- **Be thankful each day**. Practically, this could take the form of writing a thank-you note or even just thanking someone via text, on the phone or in person for all they do for you.
- **Keep a gratitude journal and review it regularly**. This will help the feeling of gratitude to become second nature.
- **Practise positive affirmation.** This could include regularly listing and counting your blessings.

Our energy can be totally depleted by people and events. So how can you protect your mindset and energy?

Think of your brain as a muscle and give it a good workout. Repetitive tasks can dull or even damage your mental sharpness, while new challenges and activities can strengthen your brain and even make you smarter. When you find yourself in a situation that feels overwhelming or out of your control, or you are around someone who always seems to be pushing your buttons, you can use a simple practice. Ask yourself this question: 'What percentage of the way I feel right now is coming from a critical voice?' Then work on taking on that critical voice in your head that tries to tell you that you can't handle things. Work on avoiding or distancing yourself from those occasions, situations and people that are energy-sappers.

Here are some top tips for keeping your brain sharp:

- Extend and push the boundaries of your development. This could be with a new hobby or by immersing yourself in a book on a topic you are unfamiliar with.
- Feed your brain. Your brain requires good fats to function at its best.[5] Healthy fats are vital to brain health, neuroplasticity and memory. Make sure you include some of the following for optimal cognitive function: grass-fed fatty meat, grass-fed butter, avocados or MCT (a type of fat found in refined coconut oil). Coffee, green tea, blueberries and pomegranates are also brilliant as they neutralise free radicals and reduce inflammation.
- Stretch your brain, for example by playing memory games or using mnemonics. Mnemonics can help to create new associations and brain pathways to remember things, like people's names. Sudoku or

even reading about unfamiliar topics can also build neural pathways.

- Raise your eyebrows! This opens your eyes wider and can give you a slight adrenaline boost.
- Look after your body. Simple habits such as regularly moving your body and getting enough sleep can make an enormous difference to your brain's functioning.
- Keep the focus positive with positive affirmations and visualisation.
- Meditate. Aim for 10 minutes per day.

I work with many elite performers and highly successful – and happy – people from all fields. Being on top of your game and staying there requires constant evolution and tons of energy. It can sometimes feel like a pressure cooker; gratitude helps you let off steam by releasing the pressure.

Below is a list of character traits highly successful people exhibit. You can adopt some or all of these to increase your gratitude, peace and abundance. Which ones can you start to implement today?

- Let things go and forgive and forget. Just bin the past.
- See problems as opportunities in disguise.
- Do not give energy-sappers rent-free space in your brain.
- Have huge dreams, and pursue them relentlessly.

- Be kind and treat people as you would want to be treated.
- Instinctively express gratitude.
- Build great relationships.
- Understand your ego is not your amigo.
- Focus on things that make a difference, not on things that annoy you.
- Practise diaphragmatic breathing (see page 28).
- Visualise the positive, practise positive affirmation and meditate in the present.

Successful and happy people have control of their inner critic. Your monkey mind looks for reasons why you shouldn't do things, why it's everyone else's fault, why it's okay to make excuses and feel sorry for ourselves. It screams that we're imposters, that others are judging us negatively, and ultimately allows us to give up. We must push back against that critical voice and lean into, not away from, our problems; it allows us to opt out of things that it says are hard, and leads us to loneliness. Loneliness also contributes to self-harm and can even lead to an increase in suicide.[6] It was such a problem over the Covid lockdowns, to the detriment of many people's mental health.

I like to work calmly through worst-case scenarios, do what I can and let the rest be. It's all too easy to ignore issues, but if you do, they tend to get gradually worse, not better. Be the buffalo and face situations head-on.

Use your brain to find a solution to limit pain or, better yet, one where everyone wins.

Here are some additional practical tips:

- Live in the moment.
- Learn to be resilient.
- Master your energy.
- Be idle sometimes – rest is vital. If things feel overwhelming, step away and look at them later or the next morning with fresh eyes.
- Practise self-compassion.
- Challenge yourself.
- Be kind to others.

Happiness comes from choosing to be happy daily, no matter what life throws at you. We will always have ups and downs, but choosing gratitude, even in the face of adversity, will boost your baseline happiness, which in turn strengthens your closest relationships and enhances well-being. That then allows you to better take care of your physical, financial and emotional health.

STARTING YOUR GRATITUDE JOURNEY

Now you know how and why gratitude works, it's time to start incorporating it into your daily life.

- Gratitude affirmations, or 'kiss your brain'. Thank your brain and body for the wonderful work they do. Do this even if you aren't in the best health or are not totally happy with your weight or appearance. Your body loves you; it does everything it can to help you and give you the best life. Love it back, choose peace over war, love over hate. It's easy to be critical and find fault in ourselves. Remember, gratitude encourages gratitude: the more you practise it, the more you will find things to be grateful for.
- Be complimentary, even to strangers on the street – if you think their jacket is fabulous, express gratitude for it. Yes, you can be grateful for something gorgeous that visually pleases you!
- Every morning on rising, write down three things you are grateful for. According to the website Mindful: 'Gratitude is more than just a momentary good feeling.'[7] There are always things to be grateful for, even on days when you don't feel like it. On mornings when you find it difficult, think: if you have a roof over your head, food in your belly, running water and people who love you, you have a lot.
- Be optimistic about what you can accomplish, and

take small steps forward. Your speed doesn't matter, only your direction. Slowly is the fastest way to get to where you want to be! Only in hindsight can you really see your progress; when you look back, you will see that you have achieved something to truly be grateful for.

- Adopt a dog's level of gratitude! Dogs are the happiest, most grateful animals around. As soon as they see a loved one, they come immediately to greet them, tails wagging. You can feel their elation and love beaming through. If you could be as grateful as man's best friend, your happiness would skyrocket, simply because gratitude begets more gratitude and good feelings.
- Write thank-you letters to the people who have helped you along the way. Your best friend, parents, siblings. The person who gave you a shot when no one else would. The person who helped you out of a sticky situation, the people who have inspired you.
- Talk to people about what you are grateful for – a little every day. Minor adjustments can lead to big changes.
- Think of all the bad things that have happened to you and find lessons in them to be grateful for. If you can do that, you will be at peace with your past. Traumas will no longer haunt you. This is an achievable yet incredible level of liberation.
- Replace gossip with gratitude. If you catch yourself gossiping or are self-deprecating, adjust your course and mindset. Step away from the conversation

– physically or metaphorically – and just think of one of your joys. Talking or thinking about other people's problems consistently eats away at your gratitude, lowers your vibe and saps your energy!

THE GRATITUDE FLIP

I read that one route to enlightenment was to have only loving thoughts for a minimum of twelve years. A mighty feat by anyone's standards.

I decided to test this out in the context of becoming more grateful. I would reframe every judgement, criticism and negative thought I had to a positive, loving, grateful one. Whenever I judged myself or another, I would flip the thought to a compliment, or something expressing love and gratitude. To make it a really interesting challenge, I decided to do it while I was on holiday with a friend who is somewhat negative and judgemental. He often moans and criticises, to the point where he can be tough company. He is regularly annoyed by strangers' actions and has no qualms about telling them off.

So, a trip with him was the perfect time to practise the gratitude flip. Every time he judged or complained I reframed the words to their opposite. It is possible to find something you appreciate in every single person you meet. Even if you are on bad terms with someone, you can admire their grit, determination, beauty, intellect, humour, sense of style, hair or something else about their appearance. They could be a rotten person but be very good at their job, or a sport, a great driver. Everyone does some good and has something good in them.

When my friend judged strangers, commenting on their muffin tops or greasy hair, I would focus on something lovely about them. Their beautiful face or cute handbag; whatever I liked most about what I saw. I maintained this practice for a week. As time went by, it got easier and easier, which I wasn't too surprised by – as we have seen from looking at neuroplasticity (practice makes perfect), our brains are wired that way. What I hadn't anticipated, though, was how blissed out I became. By the end of the week I was walking on air. It was wonderful! My energy was high, I felt on top of the world and I was in a flow state; manifesting became much easier!

Why not give it a go? Work on flipping negative thoughts to positive ones. See how happy you are at the end. You may find it a hard practice to sustain but stick at it; it will be worth it. Consciously gratitude-flipping for a week will prove how much power your thoughts, gossiping and judgements have over your baseline happiness level. If you can become five or even ten times happier by practising a little emotional discipline, isn't it worth a try?

Aristotle said: 'If happiness is not god-sent, then it

comes as the result of a goodness, along with a learning process and effort.'

If you want to boost your spirits and energy, smile more. A study done a number of years ago found out that the act of smiling actually makes you happy, even if you're not feeling it.[8] A genuine smile has more benefits than a fake one but, to a degree, fake it till you make it really works. Participants were asked to hold a pencil between their teeth while watching funny cartoons. The pencil could be lengthwise between their teeth or hanging downwards from the tip. Try it – either way, you will be forced to smile. Other participants were asked to hold the pencil between their lips, not touching their teeth. This contracts the facial muscles, causing a frown or even a pout. The scientists hypothesised that the smiling participants would find the cartoons funnier than their counterparts.

They were correct. Even a fake smile actually makes you happier. It does make me wonder about all those people who make a 'duck face' or pout for photographs. I wonder if that expression actually makes them unhappier?

The act of smiling is linked to the production of dopamine, oxytocin and serotonin. So, smiling is even a mild antidepressant.[9]

Smiling has many more benefits, even if you are faking it!

- Smiling makes us more attractive (so I wonder – do pouts push people away?).
- Smiling relieves stress – it permeates our whole being.
- Smiling prevents us from looking tired and worn down.
- Smiling elevates our mood and helps us stay positive.
- Smiling is contagious.
- Smiling boosts the immune system.
- Smiling lowers blood pressure.
- Smiling reduces pain.
- Smiling makes us look younger.
- Smiling makes us seem successful.

Try some of the exercises above and observe what changes you see. Keep going – gratitude is something to cultivate over time; it works in accordance with the law of abundance: the more you give, the more you get. When you feel your spirits lift, add more gratitude to the mix and see what happens. The more gratitude you have, the more energy you will have, because you won't get so bogged down sweating the small stuff. Then the more peace will seek you out and the more fulfilled and happy you will be!

1 As a percentage, how much do I love myself today? I will check back in with this once a week.

2 Every day for a week I will flip a bad thought. An example is:

3 I will consciously smile a fake smile every morning for a week. Come back and write down how it made you feel.

4 Who can I write and send a thank-you note to?

5 Three bad things that have happened to me and what I can find in them to be grateful for:

6 Three things I am grateful for:

CHAPTER EIGHT

Body Voltage and Energy Cultivation

Think of your body voltage in terms of a bank account. Some things add to your energy balance and some things deplete it. In this chapter you will discover that your energy levels are dependent on your actions. This is terrific news because once you understand what enhances and saps your life force, you can adapt your behaviour accordingly.

Body voltage can pass between people, too. When someone you like flirts with you, you feel alive. Attraction and admiration fill you up. You can meet someone new and feel like you already know them; there is sometimes a kinship, be it romantic or platonic. Even a great work meeting or collaboration can leave you buzzing. Celebs often look radiant as we all project love at them every time we watch their movie or listen to their songs. All of these situations fill the receiver with photons, which are particles of light.

You have already learned some ways to cultivate and sustain your energy in the chapter on energy work in nature; this chapter will expand your wisdom further.

Body energy and life-force cultivation are nothing new; they are ancient, in fact. You may have even heard of prana or chi? Both mean life force, and luckily for us their cultivation has been tried and tested for millennia.

You will also learn which actions add juice to your battery pack and which drain you. You can already identify people who are radiators and drainers; now it's time to bring this knowledge into more areas of your life, so you can really get a handle on how to be full of energy – which along with all the other tips in this book, will help you to live your best life.

Follow the simple steps below to radically increase your energy levels fast and for free. All it takes is a little wisdom, and some adaptations in behaviour.

ELECTRONS AND ENERGY

We are electrical beings; we consume, emit and excrete energy and life force. Having tons of energy is one of the underpinnings or tell-tale signs of good health. The more energy you have naturally without the aid of stimulants, the better your health is likely to be. Energy is a resource; when you have it your body can maintain itself well. It also means that mentally and physically you have the bandwidth to make good choices – to do things like exercise, and cook healthy meals rather than eating ready meals simply because you are exhausted. The more energy you have, the more potential for joy you have; and the more potential for joy you have, the more energy you get – it's a virtuous circle!

Electrons and Negative Ions

If an atom has more electrons than protons, it's called a negative ion.[1] Negative ions are invisible, tasteless, odourless molecules that we inhale en masse from certain environments such as mountains, waterfalls and beaches. Once the negative ions reach the bloodstream, they cause biochemical reactions which work to elevate mood, boosting serotonin, helping us boost our energy and lowering stress. Studies have found that negative ions can even alleviate depression.[2] Negative ions are gases in the air that positively affect mood – because emotion is a gas! Additional benefits include increased blood flow to the brain, which results in less drowsiness, higher alertness and more mental energy.

ELECTRON DONORS

How many electrons are you depositing into your body? Electron donors increase your life force, adding to your battery bank balance. Sunshine is the ultimate electron donor. You may have noticed that when you go on a holiday somewhere sunny, you tend to have more energy. You bounce out of bed in the morning even having had less sleep, with no need for an alarm. Sunny holidays are awash with electron donors; you tend to be outside more, soaking up the sun and nature. Sunshine makes you feel great because it boosts happy hormones and vitamin D, strengthening your immune system.

So how do you get the sunny benefits when you can't fly off to somewhere tropical? Many of you may, like me, live in England, home to some of Europe's officially gloomiest cities;[3] but there are a few ways to optimise sun exposure even in grey Blighty!

- Plan around the weather. Brits are well-known for talking about the weather, so why not really embrace it and plan around it? Check a seven-day forecast and plan your meetings around it. If you can't plan your day around the weather, at least make sure you make a point of going out when you can. If you drive to work you could arrive ten minutes early and sit in the sun. If you take the bus or underground, leave plenty of time so you can disembark a stop or two early and walk the rest of the way; this has the benefits of getting your body moving as well as sun exposure. You could go for a walk in your breaks, or maybe you can be flexible with your shift and get some rays before or after work.

- At weekends or whenever you have time off, get outside. It's all too easy to live a nocturnal lifestyle and only go out at night, especially if you are a city slicker. Arrange some activities around being outside instead; perhaps a lovely walk or an al fresco meal? Limit TV binges in darkened rooms.
- Gladiators in Ancient Rome trained outside because it was believed that it gave them extra strength. If you like your sports, take them outside. Parks often have free gym equipment you can use, which will be a great change of scenery from a gym in a basement and all the artificial lighting. You might be surprised to learn that there is a strong correlation between having enough vitamin D and optimal muscle function. Increasing your sun exposure can reduce pain, inflammation and muscle weakness, while increasing muscle growth, strength, jump height, power and velocity. Sunlight strengthens your bones and helps prevent fractures. It makes you sleep more deeply, too, which allows faster recovery from exercise. That, in turn helps you to build muscles faster.
- If you do miss the sun, don't worry; some sunlight does get through the clouds, so get outside, even if it's overcast.
- If you work nights or for other reasons really can't get out much (or even if you can get outside but want to

build on the sun's benefits), you could look into a SAD (seasonal affective disorder) lamp. SAD therapy lamps are used to brighten your home, giving the impression of more sunlight. There are also LED devices that deliver red and near-infrared light (NIR) light on a biological and cellular level, which can enhance your energy production. If it's winter and you are feeling blue, you could have a short session on a sunbed. Long sessions can be damaging to the skin, but a quick five minutes will boost you.

- There are even alarm clocks that mimic sunrise by getting gradually brighter; these wake you up slowly and naturally rather than jolting you with chimes or beeps.

Walking barefoot on natural surfaces, like grass or sand, pumps up your battery. Leaning against a tree – or tree-hugging – will boost your life force, as trees donate electrons.[4] If you have never hugged a tree, I encourage you to try it; it may feel a bit odd at first, but it really does energise you. And if this proves too extreme for you, sit with your back against the tree instead with a book, or listening to music. This will give you the same electron exchange, as the tree absorbs your positive ions and gives you negative ions in exchange. Or simply go for a walk in the woods.

ENERGY HACK

Go to your garden, the local woods or forest or a park. If you are shy about doing this in public, you may want to go somewhere remote where there aren't too many people, or at a less busy time such as daybreak.

1) Turn your phone to silent or, better yet, switch it off – no headphones, no music; it's time to get at one with nature.
2) Have a stroll around the trees and see if there is one that speaks to you. Is there one you find particularly appealing? I tend to like big old trees.
3) Once you have selected your tree, give it a hug! You will experience the benefits within a few seconds, but I do recommend hugging the tree for at least 30 seconds or for as long as you want to. You may notice a boost in your energy and a quieting of your monkey mind – this is because of the energy exchange in which you are offloading positive ions and absorbing negative ions.
4) See how you feel. If you notice positive benefits, you could set yourself an intention or a habit of going out to hug trees regularly.

Hugging animals will increase your life force. A common way to make people living in nursing homes feel better is to give them a dog or a cat; studies report great health benefits to residents.[5] Of course, not all care homes allow pets; but many do offer pet therapy, where animals 'visit' and, usually along with a handler, interact with residents. Animal therapy can work wonders; interacting with animals brings joy and affection. When you hug your pet, they gift you electrons, then go outside again to gather more and bring them back to you. So, all that time spent cooing over your animal is time well spent! Pets love us, and love creates photons or light. As we've seen before, enlightenment is all about having more light – it's about light cultivation. The more love you give and receive (from people and animals), the more light and life force you will have. If you don't have your own pet, you could volunteer to walk a friend's dog, which has the additional benefits of the extra sun, or daylight, even if it's overcast, and exposure to nature. You could also pet-sit, consider getting your own pet or simply say hello to horses in fields and pet friendly dogs when you are out on a walk.

Hugging and loving animals also boosts the production of the 'hugging hormone' oxytocin, which helps to combat loneliness.

Caring for – and getting love back from – pets is an excellent way to boost your energy and add more juice to your internal batteries.

Moving water is an electron donor. The motion of the water charges it and, therefore, anyone who comes in contact with the water gets 'pumped'. If you have the opportunity to get into flowing water, take it, and deposit electrons into your battery bank balance.

Swimming in a river or the sea will boost your body's electrons. Cold-water swimming is invigorating not just because of how the water is moving but due to the temperature too. A shower energises you more than a bath. Sitting in a jacuzzi with the bubbles rolling also adds to your battery bank balance. Moving water makes you feel alive. Just think of surfing or white-water rafting, or even waterfalls: there is a certain exuberance to moving water.

Rain is, of course, moving water, which is why dancing in the rain feels so good. Storms quite literally electrify the air. The air becomes charged with electrons at the first sign of drizzle. If the storm is heavy or, better yet, 'electric' with lightning, all the better; even more electrons will be produced and available to you. When it rains next, I dare you to go outside and revel in the 'bad' weather, jumping in puddles, and frolicking in the deluge. If that's really not for you, get outside as soon as the rain stops and absorb the bountiful airborne ions. The more negative ions you absorb, the more alive you will feel and the more you will boost your battery.

ELECTRON STEALERS

Just as some things boost your electron levels and your energy, some deplete them; these are electron stealers. Still water tends to steal your electrons, depleting your energy levels. Paddling in a tranquil lake or pool is a beautiful experience in many ways, but on this level you may find it tiring.

Moving air or wind of any kind is an electron stealer. For example, you may have noticed that you feel exhausted more quickly when you go for a walk on a windy day. Riding in a convertible, too: although it's a lot of fun, you may find that you are tired when you reach your destination. If it's a particularly sunny day, though, this will be at least partially offset, since (as we have seen) sunshine donates electrons. Sitting in traffic with the roof down and no wind will tip the scales in your favour too, for the same reasons. I have a convertible car and have certainly experienced this.

All toxins steal electrons; and toxins are especially prevalent in GMO food or anything grown with pesticides. Eating organic as much as possible or, better yet, growing your own food naturally will increase your electron load. Touching the soil, and plants, as well as controlling the substrate and growing conditions, will boost your life force.

There are of course a multitude of air pollutants in our modern world, especially in cities, so it's critical to get into nature as much as possible.

The biggest electron stealer of all, though, is emotional baggage. Every time you lament on traumas you are self-sabotaging by depleting your life force significantly. Being at peace with even the worst things that have happened to you will mean that you live a happier life. You need to let go of your past to live a content life in the present. Don't let the past steal your life force today.

Make a deposit into your battery bank account daily by cultivating and adding electrons. If you want to live a long and blissful life, make a choice to avoid depleting yourself and replenish yourself instead. The more energy you have, the less minor infringements will bother you, creating a virtuous circle; so, as things bother you less, you'll spend less energy on them and so have more to spare.

It's easier to brush off irritations when you are abundant with energy. Go for a walk, get into nature, and let the past stay in the past, or it will wreck your future. Recharge your batteries whenever you can by getting into daylight, nature or moving water, or playing with pets. Avoid situations and people who sap your energy.

1 Which people fill me up when we meet?

....

....

2 For a week I will plan my work day around the weather. Come back and write down how you found it.

....

....

3 How can I bring a pet into my life?

....

....

4 Three things I can do/places I can go to get outside more during the work day:

....

....

5 What can I spend an hour doing outdoors rather than watching TV?

....

....

CHAPTER NINE

My Grand Theory of Dis-ease – Gas–Liquid–Solid

What I'm going to share with you in this chapter is the discovery of a lifetime. Like all big discoveries, some of the information here may be a lot to take in initially. Discovering my Grand Theory of Dis-ease is my greatest accomplishment, because I know that the potential it offers is limitless. You will be able to apply my theory to many areas of your life, from manifesting to weight loss to dis-ease. It truly will revolutionise your world and the way you think!

My theory works on several levels, but I'm going to talk first about food and diet; I know we've looked at this subject already, but it fits into my grand theory too.

Although I firmly believe the cause of dis-ease to be primarily emotional, diet and lifestyle play an important part, especially in our modern world. Much of the food found in supermarkets now didn't exist a hundred years or even fifty years ago. In the seventies, people were far healthier in many ways than they are today. Think back to old photos of yourself or your parents forty or fifty years ago. Most people back then were trim. I think it's very significant that processed food didn't exist in the quantity it does now. Much of what's on offer in supermarkets today is barely food; if fresh food doesn't rot, you shouldn't eat it is a basic rule of thumb. Think about that as you next look at the items in your local supermarket. There are a few exceptions to this rule: honey can last for millennia, and pickles and fermented food are also an exception because of the preservation process. The first evidence of people pickling food is from Mesopotamia in 2030 BC; pickled cucumber seeds were brought from what is now northern India to the Tigris Valley.[1] I think the ancients had significant wisdom that extends to food preservation and a deep knowledge of what was good for us. Knowledge that we are only now re-discovering. Honey is an anti-inflammatory, antibacterial agent and an antioxidant. It can be used orally to treat coughs and colds, or topically to promote wound healing and treat burns.[2]

Kimchi and kombucha have become popular in recent years due to their gut-health benefits, provided by their live 'good bacteria', or probiotics, and antioxidants. They are also said to improve immune function and aid digestion.[3]

The more chemical processes your food has gone through, the less healthy it is. I think this is because processing food depletes the food's life-force energy. Cooking from scratch is wonderful; however, if you have outsourced processing to machines, energy is lost. We have the saying 'cooked with love', meaning that if you cook food lovingly, you are projecting the gas of your positive thoughts into the food, making it potentially taste better. It might not be the best idea to cook when you are in a bad mood!

Let's consider pizza with a white dough base: the wheat for the flour is harvested, the bran or shell is removed, the wheat berry is ground into flour. The flour is then mixed with yeast and water, kneaded and allowed to prove, kneaded and proved again, before being rolled or spun out, piled with toppings and cooked.

Don't get me wrong, I love pizza! Although for these reasons, I rarely have it. I favour food that comes directly from farm to table. The closer to nature your food is, the better it is for you. I also believe that meat is vital to health; I have heard and read many fascinating stories of people who have healed all sorts of dis-eases from blindness to autoimmune issues simply by switching to a good-quality meat-based diet. If possible go for organic/grass-fed meat, not the mass-produced kind or anything processed, laden with known carcinogens. Please bear in mind that a meat-based or meat-only diet may not be for everyone; experiment and find out what works for you.

Many of the ingredients in modern foods are heavily toxic. Our bodies have no idea how to excrete them; they are 'swept under the rug', by which I mean stored as fat.[4] We can end up overloaded and overwhelmed with toxins, too busy putting out fires elsewhere, with stress and body maintenance, not to mention any other illness you may have, to be able to process the chemicals stored in our fat. You only have so much energy on a given day. If you have a highly toxic diet, your body will be diverting much-needed resources to process the poisons, so you don't feel the ill effects. Your energetic resources could be better used bolstering your immune system or on other maintenance.

Your body is a highly sophisticated biochemical machine that knows what it needs. This means it will keep consuming fuel until you give it the fuel that is necessary and appropriate.

You may have noticed that when you have had a highly nutritious meal such as organic steak with plenty of fruit/vegetables and good fats/oils, you are full for hours and feel vitalised. If you want carbs, it's best to avoid highly processed white carbs such as bread; or if you do want bread, you could bake it yourself or go for something like a baguette or fresh roll that goes stale fast. If bread doesn't go stale it means it contains chemical preservatives, toxins that won't do you any good. Avoid making starchy food the main part of your meal where possible. Fats keep you feeling full for a long time; this is your body telling you that you are satiated; not just full, but adequately fuelled with the kind of food it needs.

Processed carbs like white bread, pasta and cereals probably physically fill you up fast, but leave you feeling famished again within a few hours, whereas fats keep you full and fire up your brain.

The fewer times the food is processed, the better it tends to be for you. This may be because switching from a solid to a liquid to a gas breaks bonds and loses energy.

Solid–liquid–gas applies to more than just food and manifesting; it also applies to dis-ease. I have profound personal experience of this.

MY DIS-EASE

A few years ago, I started suffering from abdominal pain, stabbing pain that made gym training unbearable and intercourse extremely uncomfortable. I attributed the pain to an injury from a trapeze session, which was also causing pain, but that was in the intercostal muscles in my ribs. I had a ton of physio, which didn't help, and was eventually recommended to have an MRI scan to see what was going on; the scan revealed no answers. In the quest to find out what was wrong, I tried all sorts, including seeing a variety of practitioners. This was particularly frustrating as I was already an accomplished healer. Eventually, I had a uterine scan and it turned out I had an ovarian cyst. I was shocked as I rarely get sick.

In my work I use the tagline 'I dissolve dis-ease, I don't get them', so I was horrified!

After I had seen the cyst on the screen (it was quite

large, just a little smaller than a golf ball), I immediately went home and opened my copy of *Metaphysical Anatomy* by Evette Rose. I had already been using the book for work for several years but had never had reason to refer to it for myself. When I finally read it from the perspective of having a dis-ease, I almost felt 'victimised' by the words! Its precision makes reading it wholly uncomfortable. It had a positive side too, though: solving problems starts with knowing what on earth the problem is. I had been in pain for a year without answers, so knowing it was a cyst was a huge relief. I also knew that it was my emotions from an abusive relationship that had caused me to grow a cyst, and now it was time to get to work. The first sentence on ovarian cysts runs:

'Emotions such as resentment have grown out of control. You may be consumed by the unjust treatment and behaviour of others (relationship with your mother or partner).'[5]

This stung, deeply. Holy smoke, it was accurate! At the time, I was in a relationship with an irate man who would regularly have tantrums over nothing. I had made the classic healer mistake of thinking I could fix him, while all along he was destroying me. I was constantly working to pacify situations while being screamed at, and I hated it. My resentment about his erratic behaviour had caused my cyst. It's also interesting to note that his ex-girlfriend had developed an ovarian cyst while she was dating him too.

An important point here is: your trauma may not be your fault, but healing is your responsibility; in scenarios like this, getting away from the toxic people who have brought on your dis-ease is a must.

I went through every sentence of the section of the book that I found so uncomfortable and energetically neutralised the dissonance. There is some 'magic' involved here that is hard to explain through the written word; I have spent two decades enhancing and unlocking my energy system and dormant goddess abilities – abilities that I teach in my school. I went through the text, line by line, and used my advanced healing techniques – my powers – to dissolve the negative feelings around the words, sentence by sentence, until I could read it without it stinging and triggering me. To my surprise, a cloud of anger and resentment consumed me for a couple of days. Three days after seeing the scan and doing this work on myself I felt a pop, and I knew the cyst had gone; when I pressed forcefully on my abdomen there was zero discomfort.

When I went for a second scan, it confirmed what I knew: there was no sign of the cyst. The nurse was baffled.

Thoughts have matter: they are a gas; but you already know this. When you spend time with an anxious person, you may become anxious. A depressed person can temporarily transmit the blues to you. If you walk into a room after an argument, you can immediately sense the tension. We even have language for it – 'You could cut the air with a knife'. Happiness and laughter are infectious; you can 'get the giggles' with a pal, unable to stop. Emotions behave like gasses; they surround us and follow us like a personal cloud containing and irradiating what we are experiencing at the time. Places and situations can feel 'suffocating', even if there is plenty of air.

There is 'mob mentality' too – think about riots. Ordinary people get caught up in the energy of a situation and start to loot and pillage, smashing and stealing. The lighter, more positive side of the mob mentality is if you have ever attended a live sporting event or concert, or even a televised football match or other sporting event in a pub, you may have felt connected to others and uplifted, you may have found yourself becoming really involved and animated. Emotion is a gas produced by people. We emanate our feelings, and it's palpable.

In the manifestation chapter we looked at the idea that everything we bring into existence goes through three stages – gas, liquid and solid – with the first, 'gas' state, being thoughts. Thoughts cause emotions and emotions cause thoughts. In my theory, dis-eases are manifested through thought in exactly the same way that everything else is. Unresolved trauma and getting stuck in a vicious cycle of repeating negative thoughts is the gas or base matter of all dis-ease.

Dis-eases themselves come in the three states of gas, liquid and solid.

Gas-based dis-eases are thought- or emotion-based

dis-eases. A room can feel heavy with emotions, be they good or bad.

Traditional Chinese medicine tells us that depression is repressed anger. Angry thoughts with nowhere to go, situations where you did not speak up (perhaps you were unable to or were trying to keep the peace?). Your angry thoughts, just like every other emotion, have matter to them; they have to go somewhere. If they haven't exploded in a fit of rage, or in you talking them out or magically dissolving them, you may have simply bitten your tongue and swallowed your rage, pushing your pain down. Depression has a heavy feel to it, anger is very animated and alive, and depression is slowed compressed anger. All emotional dis-eases are gas-based dis-ease according to my model.

Let's look at the next category: liquid-based dis-ease. Which dis-eases do you feel behave like liquids (fluids)? How about backache? Often backache moves around, never fixed in one position. It can wander, an inch to the left, or to the right, up or down. Behaving like a liquid, cysts are quite literally balls of fluid.

How does a gas change state and become a fluid? The easiest and most common way to think about this is in terms of how steam turns to liquid water and vice versa. If you boil water in a pan with the lid on, the water (liquid) starts vibrating so fast that it becomes steam, the gaseous form of water. If you have the lid on the pan, the steam has nowhere to go and it gathers to become liquid once again.

So, if you pump enough steam into a sealed container, as it runs out of space it will become a liquid. Steam and water are the same substance; the only difference is their 'state', which means how hot and spread out they are. The molecules in gases zoom around a long way apart from each other. In liquids, the molecules are slower and more densely packed.

The 'steam' in the context of dis-ease is emotional fixation, traumas relived in the mind and/or ongoing abuse.

General backache, for example, is emotionally related to not feeling supported, lack of structure, stability and responsibility. This makes a lot of logical sense, as the back physically supports your whole body. If you feel unsupported in your marriage or other areas of your life, you may be prone to back pain.

The middle back relates to humiliation, embarrassment, feeling controlled and dominated, as well as feeling responsible for others, and confusion between what is your responsibility and what is not.

Lower backache relates to being worried about finances and a lack of structure to your monetary situation.

Which diseases fit into the 'solid' part of my theory? A great example of a solid-based dis-ease is a tumour. Tumours tend to be rock hard. How does a liquid become a solid; water become ice? It's the same process through which a gas becomes a liquid: within a confined space the molecules slow down and cool down. The water molecules in a liquid are still moving but at a slower pace than the gas. Solids are slower still – they mainly vibrate on the spot and are colder.

How does this relate to tumours? In my opinion, tumours start from traumas, something deeply upsetting that happened long ago and which you haven't managed to let go. A situation that haunts you relentlessly. Thoughts are gases and the more you think about things, the more gas you create. If not released, gas has to go somewhere.

Einstein tells us that 'Energy cannot be created or destroyed, it can only be changed from one form to another'. Emotions are simply 'energy in motion'. As the energy cannot be destroyed, it has no option but to change state. Your thoughts go somewhere and become something. The location and the category of dis-ease depend entirely on your thoughts and emotions. To find out exactly which emotions cause which dis-ease I always refer to *Metaphysical Anatomy* by Evette Rose.

In my theory, dis-ease is frozen trauma and compressed thought. I hope you find this comforting; remember, when you know what is happening, you can take steps to fix the problem. It's my view that if you are truly able to forgive and let go of your bad feelings, your health will improve exponentially. In the immortal words of Elsa in *Frozen*, 'Let it go'! – let go of anything and everything that weighs you down.

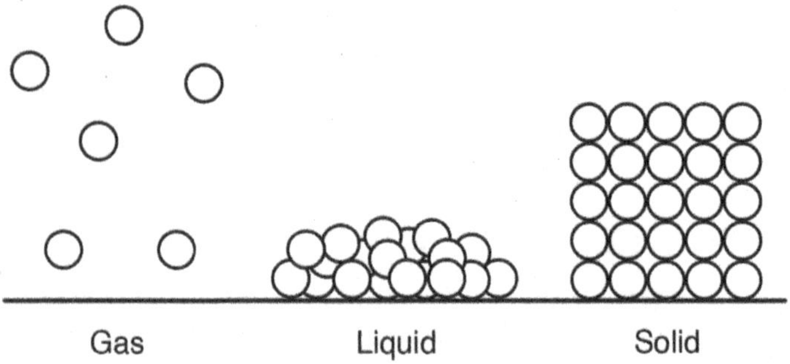

There are many concrete examples that illuminate my grand theory. Through my view of the world, here are just a few examples.

LOSING WEIGHT

One of the easiest ways to see my grand theory of dis-ease in action is weight loss. What happens when you lose weight? Where does that fat go? The fat, which is a solid, is converted to liquid water and carbon dioxide, which is, of course, a gas. If you lose, say, 10 pounds of fat, precisely 1.6 pounds turns into water, which you excrete through urine and sweat; the remaining 8.4 pounds – the majority – comes out through your lungs. To put it another way, the majority of weight lost is exhaled.[6]

This may surprise you, but almost everything you eat comes back out through the lungs. Every carbohydrate you eat and most of the fats are converted to water and carbon dioxide; the same is true of alcohol. The solid fat becomes liquid in your bloodstream, which is converted to Co_2 and exhaled (solid–liquid–gas!)

HORMONES

Hormones are another example of how the body uses gas, liquid and solid. Remember in the fight-or-flight chapter (Chapter One) when we looked at the hormones we produce and the effects they have? When you are stressed, upset or terrified – which are all emotions and thoughts, and so are all gases, as we know – you produce liquid in the form of the stress hormones cortisol, adrenaline and noradrenaline. When you are elated, blissed out, happy or in love you make, again in the form of liquid, the happy hormones oxytocin, serotonin, dopamine and endorphins. Your thoughts, therefore, instantly create or manifest liquid hormones.

TEARS

Crying is a form of stress relief; looked at in terms of my grand theory, the negative thoughts making you feel sad or upset – which, as we've seen, are a gas – are converted to water and released. The release is cathartic. Scientists have found traces of stress hormones in tears.[7]

Other studies have found that crying also stimulates the production of endorphins, which, as we know, are our happy hormones. This is an example of my theory of liquid to gas: the liquid of crying makes you feel better through these endorphins, which means it is altering your thoughts – which are gas. In addition, crying is excreting liquified trauma and heavy emotions; it releases the gaseous emotions from your energetic field in the form of tears. Liquid emotion releases the gas emotion, which is why you often feel better after a good cry.

My solid–liquid–gas theory can be mapped on to some fascinating phenomena, including swords in stones and the building skills of ancient people; it's also found in studies in the field of modern physics.

Solid–Liquid–Gas in Science and in History

Liquefying stone sounds far-fetched but we all know the story of Arthur and the sword in the stone. The question is how did the sword get there in the first place? To insert a sword into a boulder you would need to liquify the stone, then insert the solid sword.

You may have heard of Padmasambhava, who was one of the founding fathers of Tibetan Buddhism and who is said to have liquified stone and left a handprint in a rock in Yang-le-shöd, Nepal, which is a pilgrimage site.[8] Pictures are widely available if you want to see it for yourself.

You may also be aware of or have visited the sites of ancient buildings such as Sacsahuamán in Peru.[9] No one knows for sure how they were made: there is no concrete, mortar or binding material to hold the stones in place, and they are so closely cut (or melted!) that you can't even get a piece of paper between them. There are no sharp edges; the edges are rounded. They almost look like hardened wax.

How do, or did, people manipulate seemingly solid stone in these ways? It seems to me to have parallels with my theory of solids, liquids and gases changing state.

Amazingly, this phenomenon of malleable stone can be recreated in the science lab. When kept at super-cool temperatures and zapped with the world's most powerful magnet, electrons become 'quantum fluid'. This demonstrates that solid matter becomes liquid under certain conditions.[10]

This is one possible explanation (do let me know if you have another) for Arthur's adventure with the sword in the stone, the ability to place handprints in stone and the construction of enduring stone buildings with no visible joins.

THINKING YOUR HEALTH

The most important factor in health is your thinking. Thinking changes everything. Your mindset determines your choices – in every aspect of life. Take diet. Do you pick healthy or unhealthy food? I'm all for treats and the joy they bring, but not as a main source of sustenance. Choose wisely.

Change your thinking around food to change your diet and your health. If you shop in person at a supermarket, try walking around the shop by a different route so you don't just pick up the same things as always, on autopilot. Or if you shop online, delete your saved order and make a new one from scratch.

How are your boundaries? This is about changing your thinking, too; change how you think you need to be around other people. Are interactions with certain people or in particular situations making you anxious? Do you feel that people take advantage of you? Could you stand more in your power and set stronger boundaries? 'NO' is a powerful word and a complete sentence! Step away, regroup your thoughts and, when in doubt, refer back to the boundaries and spiritual hygiene chapter (Chapter Three).

Decide to walk away from negative situations or learn how to handle them better. Choose to be with people who are radiators rather than drainers.

We have seen that in my grand theory, mind fixations

– another aspect of thinking – create dis-ease. Your negative thoughts have matter, so if you if are continually upset, for example, you may well start to manifest an illness. Another way to look at it is that dis-eases are neon signs showing you where your unprocessed emotions are; working through them will improve your health in a multitude of ways. I find this liberating as it allows you to regain some control over your health and wellness. You don't need to outsource your happiness or rely on chance or others to fulfil you. Happiness is homegrown; it all starts with you!

Now you know that dis-ease is compressed emotion and frozen trauma, become the captain of your ship and start to live the life you deserve, the life you were always destined to have. Slow down and take the time to sit with yourself, free of distractions, and work out what you can do to improve your life. You have all the tools you need: taking action is the next step; freedom and happiness are achievable. Don't be bound to the traumas of your past; sit with them and release them, set boundaries and choose who you have in your life. This is your life: you are the writer, director and actor; no one can live it for you. Create a life you love. Everything starts with a thought, so create your dream life in your mind, then take the steps you need to bring it to fruition!

1 For a week I will keep a food diary of what I eat and how it makes me feel, physically, mentally and energetically.

....

....

2 Who in my life can I see negatively affects not just me but others too, and who positively affects mine and others, lives?

....

....

3 The next time I go to an event or gathering I will carefully tune in to the energy and note its quality and how it affects me. Come back and write down what you noticed.

....

....

4 What do I fixate on?

....

5 The ultimate vision board: I will create on paper a visual representation of the whole life I can see for myself.

....

....

....

Final Thoughts

I hope you have found my pearls of wisdom illuminating, even enlightening. Maybe your mind has even been a little bit blown in a paradigm shift. I hope that this book has worked and continues to work on several levels. You will have read it from the place you are at in your personal journey to self. You may wish to keep referring back to it as you progress; you may well have 'a-ha' moments whenever you look back at it.

Remember, Rome wasn't built in a day; you are a masterpiece which just needs a little tweak here and there.

Please implement changes in a sustainable way, and remember, you don't need to do everything all at once. It's easy to get excited and want it all now; I know I do! Make gradual changes and add to your routine incrementally. Notice when you could have been a little kinder to yourself or others. Pay attention to when you start to become overwhelmed, so you can adjust course before you boil over. Everything in moderation, including moderation – and my tips!

This book is aimed at helping you adapt your lifestyle so that your baseline is happier and more at peace, to boost your energy and love of life. It's designed to give you tools to steer you onto the right path for you. If the concepts here resonate deeply, I would love to have you in my tribe, dissolving dis-eases, awakening magic and boosting love; if you feel drawn to become a student, I would love to have you. The easiest way to get in touch is through my website, www.divineempowerment.com, and you can subscribe to my newsletters there. I'm very active on Instagram @Antonia_Harman as well as YouTube: @AntoniaHarman. Listen to my podcasts. My Spotify is Divinely Empowered with Antonia

Discuss the book and its concepts with friends and loved ones. You may be surprised at the response you get. Many people are quietly noticing the energetic world around them but perhaps not talking about it. Chatting about the book and its concepts will benefit you all.

Remember, selfless service or 'seva' is just about the most rewarding thing there is; I promise it will fill you with joy, as well as boost your life force and energy.

Be a bearer of light in moments of darkness and teach others how to elevate their happiness.

Happiness and kindness are contagious, so pay them forwards; it all starts with you! You are in control of your energy, health and wellness! The energy you emanate has an effect on you and on your loved ones, as well as on what you manifest in your life. Choose the life you want, the life you deserve.

In the immortal words of Glinda from *The Wizard of Oz*: 'You always had the power, my dear, you just had to learn it for yourself!'

Endnotes

CHAPTER ONE

1 https://www.mentalhealth.org.uk/about-us/news/survey-stressed-nation-UK-overwhelmed-unable-to-cope
2 https://www.imedpub.com/scientific-journals-list/effects-of-stress-on-child-iq-10960.html
3 https://www.ncbi.nlm.nih.gov/pmc/articles/PMC4212945

CHAPTER TWO

1 https://www.ncbi.nlm.nih.gov/pmc/articles/PMC6278213

CHAPTER THREE

1 https://pubmed.ncbi.nlm.nih.gov/17913417

CHAPTER FOUR

1 https://www.medicalnewstoday.com/articles/320289
2 https://pubmed.ncbi.nlm.nih.gov/20359265
3 https://gut.bmj.com/content/46/5/689.full
4 https://www.ncbi.nlm.nih.gov/pmc/articles/PMC1792397
5 https://www.ted.com/talks/robert_waldinger_what_makes_a_good_life_lessons_from_the_longest_study_on_happiness?language=en

CHAPTER FIVE

1 https://stories.uq.edu.au/imb/the-edge/inflammation/common-inflammatory-diseases/index.html
2 https://www.sciencedirect.com/science/article/pii/S1550830719305476
3 Earthing Reduces Weight Effortlessly – Intuition Physician (intuition-physician.com)
4 https://www.lung.org/blog/promising-placebo-salt-halotherapy

CHAPTER SIX

1 https://www.pnas.org/doi/10.1073/pnas.1011492107

CHAPTER SEVEN

1 https://www.youtube.com/watch?v=wZWN6lfVYtw What is gratitude

2 Marmot MG, Smith GD, Stansfeld S, et al. Health inequalities among British civil servants: the Whitehall II study. Lancet. 1991;337(8754):1387-1393. doi:10.1016/0140-6736(91)93068-k
3 https://www.health.harvard.edu/healthbeat/giving-thanks-can-make-you-happier
4 https://www.apa.org/pubs/journals/releases/psp805804.pdf
5 https://wexnermedical.osu.edu/blog/boost-your-brain-power-with-the-right-nutrition#:~:text='%20Did%20you%20know%20up%20to,important%20for%20learning%20and%20memory
6 https://www.sciencedirect.com/science/article/pii/S0165032720328706
7 https://www.mindful.org/the-science-of-gratitude
8 https://journals.sagepub.com/doi/10.1177/1745691616674458
9 https://www.sclhealth.org/blog/2019/06/the-real-health-benefits-of-smiling-and-laughing/#:~:text=When%20you%20smile%2C%20your%20brain,the%20serotonin%20is%20an%20antidepressant

CHAPTER EIGHT

1 https://www.webmd.com/balance/features/negative-ions-create-positive-vibes#:~:text=Once%20they%20reach%20our%20bloodstream,and%20boost%20our%20daytime%20energy
2 https://www.ncbi.nlm.nih.gov/pmc/articles/PMC3598548
3 https://www.statista.com/statistics/609846/total-sunshine-hours-in-england-uk/#:~:text=The%20United%20Kingdom%20has%20some,of%20more%20than%20one%20million
4 https://www.ncbi.nlm.nih.gov/pmc/articles/PMC6213340
5 https://pubmed.ncbi.nlm.nih.gov/29596708

CHAPTER NINE

1 https://pickleguys.com/the-history-of-pickles/#:~:text=The%20earliest%20known%20examples%20are,seeds%20to%20the%20Tigris%20valley
2 https://www.mayoclinic.org/drugs-supplements-honey/art-20363819#:~:text=In%20addition%20to%20its%20use,burns%20and%20promote%20wound%20healing
3 https://www.normanregional.com/blog/why-kombucha-is-good-for-your-gut#:~:text=Kombucha%20and%20other%20fermented%20foods%20are%20full%20of%20antioxidants%20and,more%20efficient%2C%E2%80%9D%20said%20Braxton
4 https://www.ncbi.nlm.nih.gov/pmc/articles/PMC6101675
5 Rose, Evette (2013) *Metaphysical Anatomy: Your body is talking, are you listening?* 2nd edn. S.l.: CreateSpace Independent
6 https://www.bmj.com/content/349/bmj.g7257
7 https://www.health.harvard.edu/blog/is-crying-good-for-you-2021030122020#:~:text=Researchers%20have%20established%20that%20crying,both%20physical%20and%20emotional%20pain
8 http://ngakma-nordzin.blogspot.com/2012/01/yang-le-shod.html
9 https://www.latinamericanstudies.org/sacsahuaman.htm
10 https://www.princeton.edu/news/2008/04/24/princeton-scientists-discover-exotic-quantum-state-matter

Further Reading

The Hidden Science Of Lost Civilisations – David Wilcock
The Ascension Mysteries – David Wilcock
Metaphysical Anatomy – Evette Rose
How To Be Well - Abby Wynne
Becoming Supernatural: How Common People Are Doing The Uncommon - Dr Joe Dispenza
The Biology Of Belief – Bruce H Lipton Ph. D
The Wisdom Of Your Cells - Bruce H Lipton Ph. D.
Fingerprints Of The Gods – Graham Hancock
The Healer – Jack Temple
The Three Waves of Volunteers – Dolores Cannon
You Can Heal Your Life – Louise L. Hay
Our Cosmic Origin – Ismael Perez
Gods Men & Monsters from the Greek Myths – Peter Lowe

Acknowledgements

I would like to thank every single person who has aided me on my journey.

To my parents, Bob and Wendy, for their help with last-minute editing and unwavering support.

To my Divine Empowerment team and The Dream Team, who believe wholeheartedly in my magic and inspire me daily.

To my PR, book agent and friend Lauren Lunn-Farrow and The Expert Agency for assisting me every step of the way. To Carolyn, Danni and Jacqui for helping me create the book.

I also want to thank David Wilcock and Evette Rose, who have been fundamental to my discoveries and spiritual evolution.

Lastly, I want to thank Lucie for creating the eureka moment which sparked my magic and changed my life forever.

yellow kite

books to help you live a good life

Join the conversation and tell
us how you live a #goodlife

@yellowkitebooks

YellowKiteBooks

Yellow Kite Books

YellowKiteBooks